Healthy Decisions

In the wake of an international pandemic, *Healthy Decisions: Critical Thinking Skills for Healthcare Executives* emerges as a crucial guide for leaders navigating the complex world of healthcare management. This thought-provoking book challenges the status quo, arguing that the success of healthcare organizations hinges not on abstract concepts like "culture," but on the concrete decisions executives make. Drawing from real-world experience with large systems like Mercy and Banner Health, specialty hospitals like Ranken Jordan Pediatric Bridge Hospital, insurance companies like Blue Cross Blue Shield, and nonprofit elder care systems, the authors provide a practical guide to help healthcare executives make the tough decisions they can't afford to get wrong.

With more than eight decades of combined consulting experience with diverse healthcare organizations, the authors present a compelling case for the paramount importance of decision-making in healthcare leadership. They argue that executives must embrace the messy, pragmatic reality of running healthcare organizations. This book offers a roadmap for healthcare leaders who want to move beyond vague discussions of culture and focus on the specific, high-stakes decisions that shape the climate of their organizations. *Healthy Decisions* offers a fresh perspective on organizational climate, asserting that it's shaped by a series of daunting decisions, not nebulous factors. The book provides invaluable insights into:

- The pitfalls of using "culture" as a convenient excuse for organizational failures
- The important role of well-developed analytical thinking skills in effective leadership
- Strategies for making difficult decisions more consistently, quickly, and accurately
- Real-world examples and research findings that illuminate the path to better decision-making
- The dispassionate thinking skills needed to assess risks and tradeoffs effectively
- How to inspire teams to embrace change, disruption, and innovation

This essential roadmap equips healthcare executives with the tools to unlock their decision-making potential, avoid the traps of indecision, and ultimately improve the health of their organizations. Whether you're a seasoned healthcare leader or an aspiring executive, *Healthy Decisions* will transform your approach to leadership and organizational success in an increasingly uncertain world.

Healthy Decisions
Critical Thinking Skills for Healthcare Executives

Linda Henman, Ph.D.
Deborah Perkins, FACHE

Routledge
Taylor & Francis Group

A PRODUCTIVITY PRESS BOOK

Designed cover image: T&F

First published 2025
by Routledge
605 Third Avenue, New York, NY 10158

and by Routledge
4 Park Square, Milton Park, Abingdon, Oxon, OX14 4RN

Routledge is an imprint of the Taylor & Francis Group, an informa business

ISBN: 9781032980683 (hbk)
ISBN: 9781032980713 (pbk)
ISBN: 9781003596912 (ebk)

DOI: 10.4324/9781003596912

Typeset in Minion
by codeMantra

Contents

SECTION TWO   Execution

SECTION THREE Talent

SECTION FOUR Build Exceptional Organizations

Preface

The global pandemic taught numerous lessons—the most important one: When healthcare executives make good decisions, little else matters. When they refuse to make decisions or show a pattern of making bad ones, *nothing* else matters. Healthcare executives should hear this as a clarion call that awakened us all to the fact that we can no longer afford the short-sighted luxury of considering decision-making a passive, pristine process. It's not. It's messy.

How did we fall into the trap of thinking of healthcare organizations in philosophical rather than pragmatic terms? Maybe when executives and boards started shying away from the difficult decisions, preferring to think of their organizations in abstract, ethereal terms that some like to call "culture." Explaining the culture of a hospital started as a well-intended attempt to understand how humans work together, but it gradually morphed into a La Brea Tar Pit, where good intentions go to die amid all the dinosaurs and fossilized specimens of organizational decisions.

Blaming failed mergers and acquisitions on "incompatible cultures" hastened the formation of the trap. Executives blame "culture," but, in truth, underdeveloped critical thinking skills—those abilities that allow us to discern—deserve more blame. Soon, *patterns* of bad judgment, those things that don't work but that people feel loathe to change because "we've always done it that way," emerge. The trap takes the form of anti-learning, anti-change, and eventually, anti-success.

A paradox emerged. On the one hand, most agree that this trap compromises effective performance. On the other hand, healthcare executives devote too little attention to *preventing*, *avoiding*, or *managing* the trap. Healthcare executives need *new* ways of thinking about the environment of the hospital, ways that will help them design and implement interventions that reduce or eliminate problems, not perpetuate them.

Healthy Decisions presents an amalgamation of what we have observed—and, in many cases, helped create—in our more than 80 cumulative years of consulting with large healthcare systems like Mercy and Banner Health, small specialty hospitals like Ranken Jordan Pediatric Bridge Hospital, and nonprofit elder care systems like Christian Homes. Our in-the-trenches experience spurred us to arrive at this premise: *To position healthcare organizations for more success, executives must make difficult decisions more consistently, more quickly, and more accurately, and they all depend on advanced critical thinking skills.*

The stories and research focus on real people and map the journey to making tough calls and identifying the key roadblocks to success. Some chapters explicitly explain "how-to," while others teach lessons in a more narrative fashion. Our stories will help you overcome what author James O'Toole aptly characterized as "the ideology of comfort and the tyranny of custom."

About the Authors

Dr. Linda Henman, Ph.D., the Decision Catalyst®, is one of those rare experts who can say she's an advisor, consultant, speaker, and author. For more than 40 years, she has worked with senior leaders in mid-sized companies that have revenues of about $30 million and with executives of very large companies that gross more than $30 billion, like Tyson Foods. In fact, Linda was one of eight succession-planning experts who worked directly with John Tyson after his company's acquisition of International Beef Products, one of the most successful acquisitions of the 21st century. Some of her major healthcare clients include Barnes Jewish Hospital, St. John's Mercy Health Care, SSM Healthcare, The Clinical Laboratory Management Association, Ranken Jordan Pediatric Bridge Hospital, Banner Health, Christian Horizons, and several insurance companies, including Blue Cross Blue Shield.

In all cases, Linda helps those in the C-suite make decisions they have to get right because they just can't afford to get them wrong. Executives like John Tyson hire her to help make sure a merger or acquisition goes smoothly. Or, the board of directors might hire Linda to help them select a new CEO, or a senior leader might need Linda's help in formulating an aggressive growth strategy.

In her more than 40 years in business, she has never had a deal fail. That means her clients made money after the M&A deal; the CEO she recommended stayed in place and succeeded; and the growth strategy helped the company expand as much as they aspired to.

Linda owes her success to her ability to influence the pivotal decisions that ultimately explain a company's success. For example, too often leaders approach an M&A deal from a technical perspective, forgetting that people and culture clashes will often cause a deal's demise. Or, when selecting a new CEO, the current CEO often hires a clone, even if the organization of the future will need someone significantly different. When setting strategy, too often, organizations do more of what they've always done, which seldom works either.

Linda takes a different approach. By combining her experience as an organizational consultant with her advanced education in business and psychology, she offers her clients solutions that are pragmatic in their approach and sound in their foundation.

Deborah Perkins, FACHE, MBA, after more than 40 years in hospital administration, joined Henman Performance Group in 2021 to provide leading-edge financial and operational consulting for hospitals, healthcare institutions, and all providers of patient care. For more than four decades, she has worked with large hospital chains like Banner Medical Health System and University of Maryland Medical System, a medium-sized hospital in Reno, and smaller hospitals in St. Louis and Illinois, resulting in millions of dollars of cost-saving changes.

Debbie specializes in making sure clients don't leave money on the table for services for which they should have been paid if the proper documentation had been completed. That means she quickly identifies both revenue growth opportunities and reimbursement threats. As a trusted advisor, she has helped hospital executives with decisions about margin improvement, case mix, reducing/eliminating denials, and increasing physician and patient satisfaction. By assisting CEOs in developing strategies to maximize revenue, her clients have been able to optimize clinical documentation and coding practices.

Debbie received a Bachelor of Science in Business Education from Southern Illinois University at Carbondale, a Bachelor of Arts in Health Information Administration from Hillcrest Medical Center in Tulsa, and an MBA from Pepperdine. In addition to having earned certification with the Registered Health Information Administration (RHIA) and Certified Professional in Healthcare Quality, she holds the designation of Fellow in the American College of Healthcare Executives and the American Health Information Management Association. In addition to serving on and presenting to several hospital associations, committees, and councils, she was elected to the Board of Directors for the American Health Information Association.

Her academic credentials, continuing education, and experience in most non-clinical areas of the hospital equip Debbie to increase a hospital's case-mix, which results in millions of dollars of revenue, reduce denials below the state average, improve clinical documentation so facilities are paid what they are owed, and implement effective Clinical Documentation Integrity programs to include internal and external audits.

Her past performance proves her commitment to empowering hospital executives to achieve their boldest vision through dramatic strategies. Her processes and procedures provide a framework for uncovering every cost-saving opportunity, thereby improving the financial health of the hospital so it can continue to offer exceptional patient care.

Section One

Strategy

Strong Strategy

Future at expense of today	**Competitive Advantage**
• Clear vision of future	• Proven track record of success
• Weak plans for execution	• Clear direction
• No assigned accountabilities	• Strong plans for execution
Unclear Tactics	*Clear Tactics*
Laurel resting	**Instant gratification**
• Past success but no commitment to future	• Strong short-term goals
• Failure to ask, "Is this still worth doing?"	• Well planned implementation
	• No clear vision of future

Weak Strategy

DOI: 10.4324/9781003596912-1

In most hospitals, you'll find more people who understand how to run fast than there are people who can decide which race they should enter...more people with well-honed skills for producing results in the short run than visionary strategists. Certainly, you need both to succeed, but most organizations are replete with those who can plug ahead and lack those who can *plan* ahead; the competition, however, is more likely to outmaneuver you strategically than to outperform you tactically. Your tactical "to-do list" (plugging away) will often keep you in the game today, but only a clear strategy can ensure your success tomorrow. Therefore, as the executive, you must understand the nature of strategy, embrace the changes it brings, set priorities for achieving what your competition can't match, and choose the right people to drive your vision. Only then will you outwit your rivals and claim your unique position.

What is strategy? Simply put, it's *what* you want to do in the future. Every organization is headed somewhere. Too often, however, that direction is not the result of a conscious choice. Instead, leaders engage in *perceived* potential, reactive decision-making, or short-term gains designed to placate shareholders and analysts.

Conversely, an effective strategy provides a way to create and capture value while serving the patient. It offers the winning formula for an organization's purpose, direction, goals, and standards: the organization's mission, vision, and values. People often talk about mission, vision, and values as if they were all the same thing, but we should think of them distinctly; each plays a complementary but separate role in the success of any strategy.

Successful healthcare leaders serve as the architect, steward, and guardian of the strategy. The job cannot be outsourced, completed, or scheduled. It is the most uncertain thing leaders do because it involves *speculation* about unknowns and requires a journey into murky waters. Coupled with hiring and developing talent, however, it ranks as the most important thing they do...and makes success more certain. Effective strategy formulation concentrates actions and resources on critical issues, gains commitment, provides a rationale for allocation of resources, enhances communication, and increases your chances of not just surviving but thriving in your industry. We typically encounter a threefold problem among my clients relative to strategy:

1. They confuse strategy with tactics.
2. They don't hire enough strategic thinkers who can handle the situational and episodic nature of strategy.
3. They make strategy an annual event, not an ongoing process.

Strategy is "what" you want to do, not "how" you'll do it. It involves setting the destination for the organization, not planning the way to get there. In fact, premature tactical planning often kills strategy development because planning, by its nature, works bottom up; strategy functions top down. Planning relies on facts, operations, and budgets, whereas strategy demands the *synthesis* of these data and creative thinking about how to gain a competitive edge. Obviously, both strategy and execution are important, but too many executives mistakenly concentrate on the tactics before they have a clear strategy. Strategies are few; tactics are many. Strategy comes first, tactics second.

In the past decade, however, many healthcare organizations have confused operational effectiveness and its merits with strategy. Generic solutions, best practices, and benchmarking cannot succeed in the long run because the competition can easily replicate them, and using them overlooks the reality that each organization is a unique system.

Successful healthcare organizations that embrace systems thinking tend to be more strategy driven. They separate themselves from the herd behavior that drives organizations to imitate one another to be all things to all patients. Continuous improvement in activities is not the enemy of strategy. In fact, it is essential for achieving superior performance, but it isn't enough. Leaders need to go beyond the orchestration of operations to *define your organization's matchless position* and make tough calls about trade-offs. You can't import your strategy from another organization because your system is inimitable. Instead, you must define your uniqueness and leverage it in new ways, the only path to a competitive strategy.

To limit servitude to the past, try asking the critical question: "If we did not already do this, based on what we know today, would we start doing it?" If the answer is "no," stop the initiative; curtail it sharply; or limit resource allocation to it. Then, you'll be able to respond to *today's* demands and to commit today's resources to *tomorrow*. Deciding what you will *not* do often becomes as important as deciding what you *will* do. Sometimes, this means a change in strategy; often, it requires a change in tactics; and occasionally, it even demands an entirely different strategy, because, in fact, there may not always be a market for the world's best horse-drawn buggy or even an effective buggy-whip.

Successful strategies rely on leaders making good decisions—not to avoiding mistakes. Strategy looks to the future, which, by its nature, is unpredictable. Your most successful strategies will align commitments that you have to make *now* with future uncertain, unpredictable circumstances. No one knows what those circumstances will be, and the future is fickle. Successful healthcare executives *do* make mistakes, often significant ones, but they keep a strategic perspective. Therefore, the most successful leaders are curious about tomorrow. They leverage their organization's competitive advantage and build on a position in the industry that competitors cannot readily replicate.

Usually, a growth strategy exists for a limited period, but sometimes, an organization identifies *expansion* as a long-term objective. Among all other influences, the desire to grow has one of the most dramatic, often hazardous effects on strategy. Limits and trade-offs take a back seat to the desire to escalate, increase, or expand. The low-hanging fruit of growth opportunity is truly tempting. Therefore, *perceived* opportunities for growth tempt leaders to go in new directions—paths that can blur uniqueness, trigger compromises, and undermine competitive advantage. Adding shiny new services is both alluring and appealing, but doing so without screening these opportunities or adapting them to your strategy also invites trouble.

That's *not* what happened at the Cleveland Clinic in Ohio, however. We will refer to the Cleveland Clinic throughout this work because it serves as a lighthouse for other healthcare organizations. The Cleveland Clinic, a non-profit academic medical center renowned for its innovative patient care and medical research, has aggressively expanded its footprint *nationally* and *internationally* through partnerships, affiliations, and acquisitions over the past decade.

That shouldn't imply that Cleveland Clinic hasn't experienced some bumps along the way. In 2022, Cleveland Clinic reported operating revenue of $12.1 billion, an increase of 8.5% over 2021. This reflected both its geographic expansion and increased patient volumes. However, in 2022, it faced some financial pressure from rising labor and supply costs from the pandemic. Its operating income declined to $281 million in 2022, compared to $571 million in 2021. Despite these setbacks, the clinic continues to flourish. Why when so many others fail? Their strategy formulation considered *awareness* of the environment in which the organization exists and *consciousness* of the impact of actions being considered for the next year or two.

The challenge of the executives is to offer a disciplined approach—an intellectual framework to guide decisions and serve as a counterweight to the quick and easy fix of unfettered growth. This requires an examination of industry changes and patient needs the organization will respond to and which ones it will reject. Penetrating existing markets and reinforcing the hospital's position help to maintain distinctiveness while squelching their competitors, distraction, and ill-advised compromise. Of course, major changes in the industry may require an organization to change its strategy, but taking a new position must be driven by the ability to find *new* trade-offs and leverage a *new* system of complementary activities.

Although today's uncompromising, competitive environment leaves you little choice other than to develop a disciplined approach to improving strategic performance, how should you do that?

Strategy distinguishes "what" you're trying to do from "how" you'll do it. Concentrate on "what." "How" comes later. *What* determines the overarching goals for the hospital, and *how* you'll reach that goal addresses the tactics (metrics) you'll set to establish movement toward achieving that goal.

Strategy should focus on *change*, not corrective action. Strategy allows you to exploit the unexpected, make the most of opportunities, and innovate your way to success, but it doesn't allow for stagnation, scapegoating, or excuse making. Identifying these critical aspects of strategy formulation allows you to take the first step; having the right people to do them allows you to take the second.

Understanding your organizational direction and the innovative nature of strategy, accepting the risks associated with making future-based decisions, and identifying and developing talent are all essential for ensuring you have a strong enough strategy to drive operations. But you also need to take the time to engage in a strategy-setting process. As Dwight Eisenhower pointed out, "Our plans may be useless, but the process is indispensable." The *process* of walking your team through a strategy session creates focus and discipline, two of the hallmarks of successful organizations.

"Strategic," one of the most overused and misrepresented words in today's organizations, denotes anything executives consider important. Yet *true* strategy is limited to those situations that are likely to affect *critical* outcomes. Strategy identifies your competitive advantage, something you can do that rivals cannot match. It defines the nature of your organization, impacts financial performance, and guides your choices. Done well, it allows you to survive in a jungle where others perish, not only to endure but to prosper in the fickle future that lies ahead.

1

Set the Compass for Decision-Making

Every organization is headed somewhere. Too often, however, that direction is not the result of a conscious choice. Instead, leaders engage in *perceived* potential, reactive decision-making, or short-term gains designed to placate shareholders and analysts.

Conversely, an effective business strategy provides a way to create and capture value while serving the customer. It offers the winning formula for an organization's purpose, direction, goals, and standards: the organization's *mission, vision, and values.* People often talk about mission, vision, and values as if they were all the same thing, but we should think of them distinctly; each plays a complementary but separate role in the success of any strategy.

WHY DO YOU EXIST?

In 2001, Linda worked with the leaders of a family-owned business to help them set their strategy for the next year. In their first meeting, they told her they were eager to have a discussion of execution because they wanted to set up a two-day seminar during which each officer of the company could identify a clearly articulated goal and timeline, both of which would be used to evaluate his performance at the end of the year. Linda assured them she would have that discussion, but first, she asked to see a copy of their mission and vision statements. Looking confused and more than a little annoyed, the father said he thought they were somewhere around there in a framed picture, and the son was pretty sure they had hired a company to put them on some mouse pads that they had used a year or

DOI: 10.4324/9781003596912-2

so ago. But neither father nor son could tell Linda what the mission and vision were!

At one time, they had written and wordsmithed a mission and vision statement, but clearly, these were no longer serving as the foundation for their strategy formulation, nor apparently, even for their desk accessories. These owners, unfortunately, represent the mindset we frequently encounter. Too often, leaders assume that simply creating (or having a consultant create) and distributing a mission statement will accomplish something important.

As Linda explained to them, before taking any steps to formulate a strategy, they should have a clear understanding of the mission and of their organization. A mission statement should play the same role in your organization that the Holy Grail did in the Crusades. Your mission defines your *reason for being*, the touchstone against which to evaluate strategy, activities, and expectations for overcoming the competition. Without one, you will diffuse resources, enable individual units of the organization to operate in silos, create conflicting tactics, and confuse customers, suppliers, financiers, and employees. Conversely, when you have a well-articulated sense of purpose, you will build a firm foundation that provides clear guidance for all significant decisions and establishes a point of reference for setting strategy and planning its execution. A mission statement answers these questions:

Why do we exist?
What is our business?
Who are our customers?
What do our customers value?

In addition to defining the organization's identity, the mission guides its development over time. Although it should be resistant to capriciousness, as the external landscape changes, leaders must tweak the mission statement as they recognize how to translate purpose into practice.

During a recent speech to hospital executives, when Linda asked an audience of 200 people from different organizations to recite their mission statements, she saw bewilderment and discomfiture. Three of the 200 hands proudly shot up to proclaim the executive of that company could remember the mission statement, but the other 197 sat stoically. Yet, when she asked these *same* people to tell me what's on a Big Mac, the entire audience recited, "Two all-beef patties, special sauce...." In other words, a commercial that has not been on TV for more than 20 years stayed in their memories more prominently than their own mission statements!

If you're like most of that audience, you are missing a basic element of your strategic direction. How can your mission serve as the foundation of your strategy and help you know where you're going if you and your people don't know what it is and how it can help you define your vision?

UNDERSTAND THE DEMOGRAPHICS YOU SERVE

Bellevue Hospital Center in New York City offers an example of a hospital making changes to better honor its mission—to serve its demographics. Bellevue, as one of the oldest public hospitals in the United States, has a long history of serving a diverse and often underserved population. Over the years, the hospital has implemented various initiatives to meet the needs of its community better.

Decision-makers at Bellevue established specialized clinics and programs tailored to specific demographics within its patient population. For instance, Bellevue developed clinics focused on serving immigrant and refugee populations, providing *culturally sensitive care* and access to *interpreters*. Additionally, the hospital introduced programs addressing the unique healthcare needs of LGBTQ+ individuals, offering inclusive services and staff training to create a welcoming environment.

Bellevue also enhanced its outreach efforts to engage with communities across New York City. This included hosting health fairs, workshops, and educational events in neighborhoods with high concentrations of underserved populations. By actively reaching out to these communities, Bellevue aspired to increase awareness of available healthcare services and encourage preventive care. Bellevue also implemented *recruitment strategies* to hire staff who reflect the diversity of the patient population. This not only helped improve cultural competency within the hospital but also fostered trust and rapport between patients and healthcare providers.

Through these changes and initiatives, Bellevue Hospital Center demonstrated a commitment to better serving its diverse demographics by providing culturally competent care, fostering inclusivity, and addressing the specific healthcare needs of its community—all aspects of their mission.

HAVE A CLEAR VISION

The global pandemic confirmed what we already suspected: there's no "normal" anymore. Gone are the days of organizations formulating strategies for the next 20, or even ten years. Here to stay is the reality that a vision must exist, but it must be flexible and tight. Leaders stand on firm ground when they plan for a year, but after that, the vision begins to blur. However, formulating a plan for the near future will build confidence among stakeholders that decision-makers have a blueprint for how the hospital will live its mission into the future.

As you formulate your plans for the future, your vision statement should be a clear picture of what you intend to do and what you will commit to do. This concise statement defines what success will look like in one, three, and five years—but not much beyond that. A well-crafted vision statement should include a stretch goal that challenges everyone to become. Vision statements should also include a definition of focus and a timeline for execution.

Once again, the Cleveland Clinic offers an example of how an organization defined its direction based on a *very specific vision* of where it wants to be in the near future. The Cleveland Clinic rolled out "Vision for 2024," its ambitious roadmap to solidify its position as a global leader in healthcare, several years before the target for completion. In addition to growing organically, they sought to do and did do the following:

Led in Patient Experience
Implemented unified electronic health records across its entire enterprise
Leveraged digital technologies like virtual visits to enhance patient access
Designed new facilities that promote improved patient experience, efficiency, and integration of care
Established a Global Center for Pathogen Research & Human Health

Invest $500 million in innovations like genomics, immunotherapy, and digital health platforms

Improved access and culturally competent care for underserved populations

With very specific growth targets and initiatives tied to its priorities, Cleveland Clinic's 2024 vision provided a comprehensive roadmap to extend its clinical, research, and educational excellence into new communities in the years ahead.

Vision statements help you decide where you're going, a critical first step in formulating strategy. It defines something significant you want to do in the future; it inspires, motivates, and challenges. When used in conjunction with your mission and values, your vision says, "This is where we are going and as we do, this is how we will conduct ourselves."

CHANGE STRATEGY BUT NOT MISSION

Mayo Clinic's primary mission is *"to inspire hope and contribute to health and well-being by providing the best care to every patient through integrated clinical practice, education and research."* Historically, Mayo focused on running an integrated practice centered around its campuses in Rochester, MN, and a few other cities. However, in 2010, Mayo updated its strategy to expand its reach beyond its core hospitals.

In 2011, Mayo launched the *Mayo Clinic Care Network* to share its knowledge and expertise with other healthcare providers. Rather than owning/operating these member hospitals itself, Mayo provides them with access to its research, clinical care protocols, and consulting services. This allowed Mayo to have a broader impact in improving care quality at many hospitals beyond its walls, without deviating from its *non-profit integrated model*. The network has now grown to more than 40 member organizations across the United States and internationally. Two years later, Mayo launched this program, offering web-based health coaching services directly to consumers.

Leaders at the Mayo Clinic recognized that its mission encompassed promoting overall health, not just treating illness. While a departure from its traditional care delivery model, the new expanded services aligned with Mayo's mission of contributing to societal well-being through preventive health education.

While evolving its approach, these strategic initiatives stayed true to Mayo's core mission—using its knowledge and expertise to enhance the quality of healthcare delivery and promote better health for patients everywhere, not just within its walls. The strategy continues to morph and change as the system evolves, but leaders have never lost sight of their mission and core values.

KNOW WHO WOULD MISS YOU IF YOU WENT AWAY

Kaiser Permanente, one of the largest not-for-profit integrated healthcare systems in the United States, has a mission "to provide high-quality, affordable health care services and to improve the health of our members and the communities we serve." Staying true to this mission of providing accessible, affordable care, Kaiser has made some pioneering moves to help those who would miss them most if they went away, people who want to go beyond healing:

- Kaiser has heavily invested in *preventive medicine*, health education, and proactive management of chronic conditions. This aligns with its goal of improving community health overall rather than just treating illness.
- Kaiser's *prepaid insurance* model, combined with its owned hospitals/clinics, allows it to control costs across the full care continuum. Profits get reinvested rather than paid to shareholders.
- Kaiser was an early leader in implementing an *advanced electronic health records system* across its entire network in the 1990s and 2000s to improve care coordination.
- To promote health and prevent disease, Kaiser has actively encouraged *plant-based diets*, including making them the default for patient meals.
- Aligned with its community health mission, Kaiser has launched initiatives to raise *awareness about gun violence* as a public health crisis.

While some of these decisions, like limiting services to Kaiser members only, were controversial, they reflected Kaiser's commitment to an integrated, *prevention-focused* model of healthcare delivery. Its non-profit status gave it the flexibility to prioritize community health over profits.

Occasionally, we remind healthcare clients that "not for profit" is a tax designation, not a goal. Even the most dedicated employees can't keep a healthcare organization afloat if it's operating in the red. Yet, these same clients remind *us* that the organization wouldn't exist at all if they lost track of the mission. Obviously, margins and mission must march in lockstep precision to create a successful organization. Here are four ways to do that:

1. *Employee Engagement*: A mission that inspires and motivates employees leads to higher levels of engagement and productivity. This increased productivity positively affects the company's bottom line, contributing to improved margins.
2. *Value Alignment*: A well-defined mission statement communicates the core values and purpose of a company. When an organization's mission aligns with its values and goals, it attracts patients who seek care from people who reflect their own beliefs.
3. *Brand Loyalty*: A strong mission builds brand loyalty. When patients feel a deep connection to an organization's mission, they remain loyal to the brand over the long term. Loyal patients return when they need more treatment, and they refer their friends and family to the organization they trust, allowing the company to maintain higher margins.
4. *Cost Efficiency*: A mission that emphasizes efficiency, innovation, and sustainability drives cost-saving initiatives within the organization. By reducing waste, optimizing reimbursement processes, and adopting sustainable practices, a healthcare facility can lower its operating costs, which in turn improves profit margins.

A well-crafted mission statement that aligns with the values and goals of both patients and caregivers drives cost efficiency, brand loyalty, and employee engagement—everything contributing to financial success.

CONCLUSION

The mission of a hospital is critically important to guiding its overall strategy and decision-making primarily because it defines the fundamental purpose of the hospital and clarifies the core values that will define its success. The mission is a kind of guardrail for strategy—a balustrade for ensuring initiatives align with the organization's responsibilities to the communities it serves.

When a hospital faces limited financial and staffing resources, a clear mission helps to establish priorities and guide the appropriate allocation of investments that directly advance its objectives and community impact. A distinctive mission can also serve to differentiate a healthcare organization from its competitors and help them shape a unique value proposition relative to other regional providers.

To unify stakeholders and provide a rallying flag that does more than serve as a pretty poster in the foyer or the printing on mouse pads, the mission must be *known, lived, and revisited frequently.* Only then will it serve to maintain public trust and shape the behaviors within its workforce. While essential, financial viability does not play the role it does in a typical corporation. The mission keeps strategy centered on *societal health needs* rather than just economic objectives. Losing that mooring can quickly compromise a hospital's integrity and public purpose.

2

Define Targets for Effective Outcomes

On August 6, 1926, on her second attempt, 19-year-old Gertrude Ederle became the first woman to swim the 21 miles from Dover, England, to Cape Griz-Nez across the English Channel, which separates Great Britain from France. Ederle entered the icy waters at Cape Gris-Nez in France at 7:08 a.m. She started that morning in unusually calm waters, but twice that day—at noon and 6 p.m.—squalls impeded her progress. Ederle persevered through storms and choppy waters, and, finally, at 9:04 p.m., after 14 hours and 31 minutes in the water, she reached the English coast, becoming the sixth person and *first woman* to swim the Channel successfully, battering the previous record by two hours.

Twenty-four years after Ederle's success, Florence Chadwick broke long-distance swimming records for women...*and men.* In 1950, Chadwick crossed the English Channel faster than any other woman in history. Two years later, Chadwick did something *else* she'd never done before.

Setting a different goal for herself and looking for an even greater challenge, Chadwick set her sights on a longer swim, the 26 miles between Catalina Island and the California mainland. On July 4, 1952, she slid into the ice-cold water off Catalina Island and began the long journey toward California's coastline.

Shortly after she began the swim, Chadwick began to feel nauseous and had trouble breathing. As her crew discovered, one of the boats had been leaking oil. They removed the offending boat, and Chadwick paddled on, stroke after laborious stroke.

Fifteen hours later, another element threatened her attempt at making history: a thick, heavy fog set in on the bay. Chadwick couldn't see her

DOI: 10.4324/9781003596912-3

support boats, much less the land ahead of her, and as the minutes passed, the fog grew denser and denser. The water temperatures changed, and the humidity caused her breathing to become more difficult. Chadwick feared she was swimming in circles, and she began to lose hope. Finally, in desperation, Chadwick did something she'd never done before. She asked her safety crew to pull her into the boat.

Chadwick soon discovered she had stopped swimming less than *1 mile* from the California shore. She had swum 25.5 miles, only to quit with a half mile to go. Later that day, Chadwick explained that she'd quit because she couldn't see the coastline. *She couldn't see her goal, and she lost hope.* Too many things, especially the fog, had complicated her journey and distracted her.

Two months later, she tried again. Although she found the fog just as dense that day, she kept going. She finished in 13 hours and 47 minutes, breaking a 27-year-old record by more than two hours, and became the first woman ever to complete the swim.

Chadwick had determined a clear way to measure her success: She wanted to swim between Catalina Island and the California coastline. But during her first attempt, she had *not* developed a plan for dealing with the unexpected fog.

What do these stories of great swimmers with clear goals teach? First, *complexity* and *clarity* seldom march together. Complexity compromises clarity and creates unnecessary distractions. Ederle had a simple goal: swim the English Channel. Some weather conditions interfered with that goal, but she pressed on because she knew what she wanted to achieve. Chadwick encountered some unexpected challenges that complicated her journey as well, but she didn't have a plan for sidestepping the traps—at least not the first time. The fog created a barrier to her seeing the goal.

Apparently, no one else knew the coast lay a mere mile away either, or that person could have shouted that encouraging news to her. On her second attempt, however, she anticipated some of the complexities and developed contingency plans for sidestepping them. When she understood that fog might stand in the way of her achieving her goal, she developed skills to keep her from being distracted. What can healthcare leaders do to avoid being distracted by the fog in their organizations?

HAVE CLEARLY DEFINED ONE-YEAR GOALS

When exceptional individuals join in the pursuit of a common goal, miraculous things can happen. Sometimes, an exceptional leader can recast the ordinary into the extraordinary, as George Washington did at Valley Forge, but more often marvels occur when leaders have stellar talent to start with. That happened at the Winter Olympics in 1980.

The U.S. victory over the long-dominant and heavily favored Soviets quickly earned the title "The Miracle on Ice," the event many consider the greatest sports moment of the past century and what *Sports Illustrated* called "the single most indelible moment in all of U.S. sports history."

What made it miraculous? To begin with, the U.S. team entered the games seeded *7th* out of 12 teams that qualified for the games. Second, composed of collegiate and amateur athletes, the U.S. team faced a formidable opponent in the well-developed, legendary Soviet players who had won the gold in the previous four Olympics.

Even though the U.S. team faced overwhelming odds, it did not put less-than-stellar players on the ice. The romantic notion that a bunch of college scrubs felled the world's greatest team through sheer nerve and determination is both misguided and inaccurate. The United States started with star performers—even though these stars had not garnered fame or press up until the Olympic Games.

The team also had a determined coach in Herb Brooks, who spent a year and a half nurturing the Olympic team, holding numerous tryout camps before selecting a roster from *several hundred* prospects. The team then spent four months playing a grinding schedule of exhibition games across Europe and North America.

Brooks emphasized speed, conditioning, unusual tactics, and discipline, but not popularity. Known for his prickly personality and fanatical preparation, Brooks united the previous rival players—often against himself. The team shared a common enemy in the locker room as well as on the ice.

The Americans entered the games as the underdogs, but they formed a team of competitive canines. From the hundreds of hopefuls, Brooks selected the 20 players who would go on to represent the United States in the miracle. Of the 20 players, 13 eventually played in the NHL. Five of them went on to play over 500 NHL games, and three played more than 1,000 NHL games.

Scrubs? Underdogs? Second best? No, the U.S. team was nothing short of a team of virtuosos. Brooks, a talented coach and former player, united the team and produced a synergistic, miraculous effect. But before we notify the Vatican of this miracle, let's keep in mind that Brooks started with impressive raw talent.

Healthcare leaders do well when they learn lessons from sports greats. Athletic coaches never attempt to "save" players who can't produce. They cut them. These coaches know they can't win unless they put the best available players in the game. They patiently wade through hundreds of applicants to find the select few who can deliver miracles. Then, they steadfastly commit to developing the talent. It doesn't happen every time—just every four years, when the best in the world compete with other virtuosos of their ilk. Maybe we should make it happen more often in healthcare.

In healthcare organizations, unless the leader articulates a clear direction for the team, there is a real risk that different members will pursue their own agendas. The top scorers on the team may be the stars that shine the most brightly, but they and everyone else know they need the assists and defensive maneuvers of their teammates. Only through collaboration can stars win a team sport.

AGREE ON PRIORITIES

When we work with healthcare organizations, we always start with the question: "What do you want to be true a year from now that is not true now?" The answer from the senior person in the organization informs us of *what* we need to do to help and *how* we should go about doing it—the strategy and the tactics. We find that openly stating objectives sends a clear message to staff, patients, partners, and the community about what the hospital values and wants to improve; and this transparency supports *alignment* and *collaboration*.

Then, we ask our clients to assess things that may interfere with the achievement of these goals in three ways: seriousness, urgency, and growth.

Seriousness is the impact of the effects of an event. When something is crucial, it demands careful consideration, attention, and a sober approach due to its potential consequences or impact.

Urgency is the need to act with speed. Not all important things are urgent, and not all urgent things are important. The questions remain, "Do we miss a key window of opportunity if we *don't* act rapidly?" or "Will our condition quickly worsen to unacceptable levels if we don't act *now?*" Evaluate the potential consequences of failing to address the problem in a timely manner. Will the problem worsen over time, leading to more significant damage, loss, or suffering? Understanding the long-term implications of inaction can help prioritize the urgency of the response. This will require an examination of the underlying *systemic* factors that may be contributing to the growth of the problem. Addressing these root causes may be necessary for a comprehensive and sustainable solution.

Growth involves thinking about the trend of the issue. How quickly is the problem increasing or spreading? Problems that grow exponentially can quickly spiral out of control and become more difficult to manage if not addressed promptly. Consider the number of people, communities, or systems affected by the problem. Is it localized, or does it have the potential to impact a larger population or geographic area? Problems that have a wide-reaching impact may require more extensive resources and collaborative efforts to address effectively.

Setting priorities involves agreeing on whether the problem is stable, growing, or declining. That's what happened at Intermountain Healthcare, a not-for-profit healthcare system based in Salt Lake City, Utah. Intermountain Healthcare has consistently demonstrated its ability to set and achieve priorities that align with its mission of providing high-quality, cost-effective care to patients.

Some of the priorities Intermountain Healthcare has set and successfully achieved include improving patient outcomes, reducing healthcare costs, investing in preventive care and technology, and developing an engaged workforce.

By setting these priorities and aligning its resources and activities to support them, Intermountain Healthcare achieved notable successes, such as reducing hospital-acquired infections, improving patient satisfaction, and lowering healthcare costs. The organization's clear focus on its priorities and tying these priorities to metrics helped it become a leader in delivering high-value healthcare and has earned it recognition as one of the top-performing health systems in the United States.

ESTABLISH KEY PERFORMANCE INDICATORS FOR STRATEGIC OBJECTIVES

KPIs stand for Key Performance Indicators. These metrics demonstrate how effectively an organization assesses progress toward strategic personal, business, and clinical goals. Typically quantifiable, specific, and directly related to the organization's performance and success, KPIs can encompass a wide range of metrics, including financial metrics (such as revenue growth and profit margins), operational metrics (such as productivity and efficiency), customer metrics (such as satisfaction scores and retention rates). By tracking KPIs, organizations can identify areas of strength and weakness, make informed decisions, and take targeted actions to improve performance and drive success—all leading to personal and organizational effectiveness.

Clear performance indicators helped the Virginia Mason Medical Center (VMMC) in Seattle, Washington, achieve its strategic objectives. To improve patient care quality, safety, and efficiency, VMMC implemented the Virginia Mason Production System (VMPS), which is based on the Toyota Production System. Leaders at VMMC focused on reducing patient wait times, patient safety, patient satisfaction, and reducing waste.

By zeroing in on these clear performance indicators, drawing on *lean management principles*, and aligning them with their strategic objectives, VMMC achieved significant improvements in quality, safety, and efficiency and made this organization a leading example of how lean management principles can be effectively applied in healthcare settings.

KNOW YOUR COMPETITORS AND THEIR WINNING MOVES

In the late 1990s and early 2000s, the changing healthcare landscape prompted a heightened awareness of Penn Medicine's competition and the need to adapt and innovate to maintain its position as a leader in the Northeast healthcare market. Leaders at Penn Medicine recognized that they had to compete with other leading academic medical centers more directly in the Northeast, such as New York-Presbyterian Hospital, Johns Hopkins Hospital, and Brigham and Women's Hospital.

These competitors, known for their cutting-edge research, advanced medical technology, and highly skilled medical professionals—all winning moves—posed a threat to Penn Medicine. Based on their understanding of the competitive landscape, Penn Medicine set its strategy to leverage its *unique strengths* and *capitalize on growth opportunities.*

It all starts with a strong *strategic principle*—a shared objective about what the organization wants to accomplish. The strategic principle guides the allocation of scarce resources—money, time, and talent.

The strategic principle doesn't merely aggregate a collection of objectives. Rather, this simple statement captures the thinking required to build a sustainable competitive advantage that forces trade-offs among competing resources, tests the soundness of initiatives, and sets clear boundaries within which decision-makers must operate. Creating and adhering to a concise, unforgettable, action phrase can help everyone always keep an eye on the ball.

A well-thought-out strategic principle pinpoints the intersection of the organization's passion, excellence, and profitability, or in the case of not-for-profit organizations, its unique contribution. Success lies at the intersection of the three (Figure 2.1).

By understanding its competitive position and setting a strategy that leveraged its academic strengths, advanced technology, and patient-centered approach, Penn Medicine solidified its position as a leading healthcare provider in the Northeast United States and continued to grow and innovate in a highly competitive market.

POSITION YOUR SERVICES TO OUTRUN THEM

Once leaders at Penn Medicine understood their competitors and their winning moves, they quickly moved to a plan of HOW they would use the information to help them position themselves to outrun the competition through a combination of strategic initiatives that capitalized on their unique strengths and targeted key growth opportunities.

They began by leveraging *academic strengths* and their strong affiliation with the University of Pennsylvania, which allowed them to attract *top medical talent*, secure *research funding*, and drive *innovation in clinical care.* The series of decisions that led to concentrating on these three

Strategic Principle

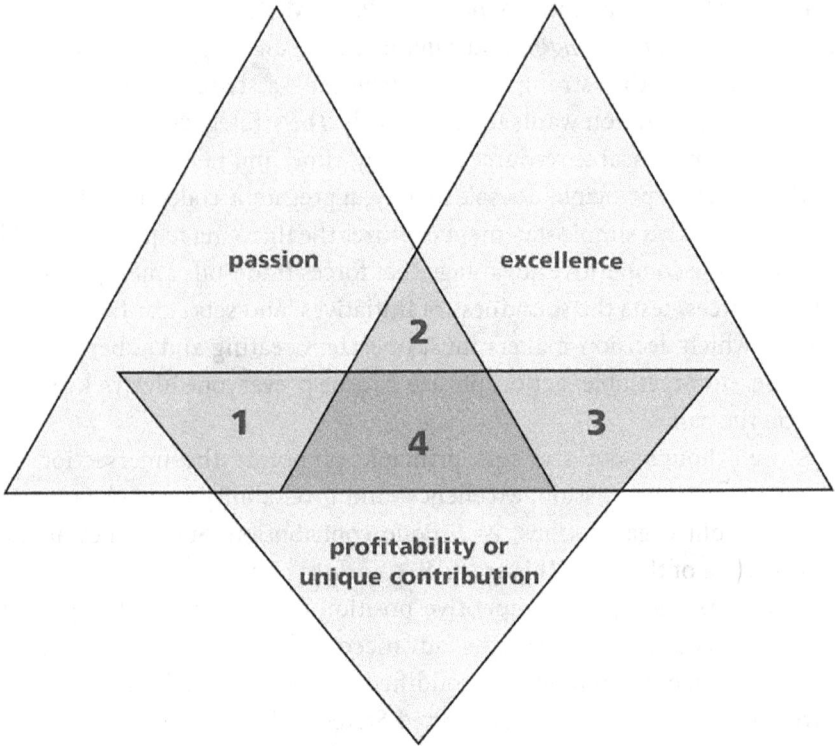

1 **Short-term success**

2 **Undisciplined orientation**

3 **Recipe for burn out**

4 **Strategic principle**—the shared objective that your organization needs and wants to accomplish

FIGURE 2.1
Strategic principle.

tactics set Penn Medicine apart from competitors who often did not have the same level of academic resources and expertise.

Penn Medicine made significant investments in cutting-edge medical technology, such as proton beam therapy, robotic surgery systems, and advanced imaging equipment. These investments allowed Penn Medicine to offer treatments and procedures that weren't available at competing hospitals, thereby attracting patients seeking the most advanced care options.

Penn Medicine actively pursued opportunities to expand its network of hospitals, outpatient facilities, and partnerships with community health providers in the Greater Philadelphia area. By increasing its geographic footprint and establishing a strong regional presence, Penn Medicine positioned itself to capture a larger share of the local healthcare market and better compete with other health systems in the area.

By developing care coordination programs, telemedicine services, and patient engagement tools, Penn Medicine differentiated itself from competitors by offering a more personalized and convenient care experience for patients. They also promoted specialty care programs in areas such as cardiology, neuroscience, and oncology. By establishing itself as a leader in these complex and high-demand specialty areas, Penn Medicine positioned itself to attract patients from a wider geographic area and compete with other top-tier academic medical centers known for their specialty care expertise.

Through targeted marketing campaigns, community outreach, and thought leadership activities, Penn Medicine reinforced its position as a premier healthcare provider, helping it to attract patients, talent, and partnerships in a competitive market and ultimately allowing the healthcare system to outrun the competition and maintain its status as a leading academic medical center in the United States.

CONCLUSION

No hospital will succeed by concentrating on the past—by focusing on the reflection in the rearview mirror. You also don't want your objectives to represent a distortion of future possibilities—like an image in a funhouse mirror. Instead, your objectives plan should be a kaleidoscope that exhibits various symmetrical patterns that reflect the loose bits of information you have aggregated. As you rotate it with new information and contingencies, new patterns and answers will appear. It is a look forward to "how's." It includes the programs your organization will complete within a year to reach your strategic objectives in four major areas: finance, customers, processes, and people. When you tie a culture of discipline to a commitment to attract and retain the best and brightest in the healthcare industry, a magical alchemy of action and results occurs.

3

Cultivate an Environment for Critical Choices

We use the word "culture" arbitrarily, citing it to explain why things don't change, won't change, or can't change. We talk about the culture of a society or country, school cultures, business cultures, culture clashes, and emerging cultures. A powerful force, culture anchors strategy and creates an environment where the best people can do their best work. It's that subtle yet powerful driver that leaders strive—often futilely—to influence. Leaders who aspire to challenge the ordinary realize they need to pay more attention to the culture they help create so they can understand it, guide it, and tie it to their strategies for growth.

So often, we encounter an executive team that seems to have it all—the whole six-pack. But they lack the plastic thingy that holds it all together. Culture is that plastic thingy. Leaders who hope to create exceptional organizations realize they must act as culture managers—people who help to create an environment where star performers can consistently and consciously challenge ordinary standards, protocols, and performance.

These leaders set the tone at the top and lead the never-ending journey to discover new and better ways to solve problems and adapt to the world around them. When something works well over a period of time, and leaders consider it valid, these vanguards lead the charge to teach behaviors, values, and ideas to new people and to reinforce them with existing employees. Through this process, people find out what those around them perceive, think, and feel about issues that touch the organization.

DOI: 10.4324/9781003596912-4

LET ETHICS GUIDE BEHAVIOR

More than 2,000 years ago, Aristotle helped us understand that ethics underpins all that defines a true virtuoso. According to him, the chief good for humanity is happiness, which, according to his philosophy, consists of rational activity pursued in accordance with virtue. In other words, living well demands *doing* something, not just *being* in a certain state or condition of integrity. It consists of those lifelong activities that *actualize* ethics and—as we now understand—create stars.

Deontology, from the Greek *deon*, which means "obligation" or "duty," defines the ethical position that judges the morality of an action based on the action's adherence to rules—choices leaders deem required, forbidden, or permitted. This school of thought posits that some acts are *inherently* ethical or unethical, irrespective of legality, pragmatics, or common practice. Philosophers commonly contrast deontological ethics with *consequentialist* ethics, that is, the rightness of an action is determined by its consequences.

So, what do virtuosos actually do? Aristotle maintained that the study of ethics seeks not to impart information but *to influence conduct.* He insisted that ethics is not a theoretical discipline: we are asking what the good for human beings is not simply because we want to have knowledge, but because we will be better able to achieve our good if we develop a fuller understanding of what it is to flourish. Therefore, what is the good?

In healthcare, difficult and controversial questions arise when we ask whether certain of these goods are more desirable than others. As Aristotle noted thousands of years ago, opinions differ about what is best for human beings. As any student of organizational theory knows, those differences of opinion pale in comparison to the debates that rage about differences in ethics, morality, and legality. Many excuse behaviors that would *ordinarily* seem wrong, but when done for the betterment of the organization, can be forgiven. (One might note that Aristotle never had a sales quota.) Similarly, legal loopholes allow for wrong-minded logic. Philosophers since Aristotle have tried to explain ethics in more practical terms, but we embrace the three criteria he posited:

The action is desirable.
The action is not desirable for the sake of some other good.
All other goods are desirable for its sake.

Virtuosos don't acquire their ethical foundations solely by learning general rules. They also acquire them through practice—those deliberative, emotional, and social skills that enable them to put their general understanding of well-being into practice in ways that are suitable to each occasion.

DEMAND THAT CLEAR VALUES GOVERN BEHAVIOR

Corporate values describe the principles and standards that guide an organization's ethical and business decisions. Organizations typically list things like leadership, integrity, quality, customer satisfaction, people working together, a diverse and involved team, good corporate citizenship, and enhancing shareholder value. While all of these are laudable, which would a successful company *not* value? A list of ideals that *any* organization would promote doesn't really distinguish your company from any other, and you're not likely to have any arguments about the importance of embracing these ideals. But how? How do you translate value on paper into value in practice? Organizational values should address thorny issues and provide a compass for navigating uncharted seas, even when the price of doing so is significant.

One notable example of a healthcare organization living its values at a significant cost is the response of various hospitals during natural disasters. In the aftermath of Hurricane Katrina in 2005, despite facing immense challenges such as flooding, power outages, and limited resources, many hospitals in the affected areas remained committed to their values of providing *care to all*, regardless of ability to pay or circumstances.

These hospitals went above and beyond to evacuate patients, provide emergency medical services, and offer shelter to those in need, even when it meant putting their own staff and resources at risk. Additionally, they continued to provide care to patients who were unable to pay for services due to the disaster, embodying their commitment to community health and well-being.

Professor Daniel Denison distinguished himself as one of the pioneers who had a keen sense of what "culture" means. Denison discovered the vast nature of culture but also concluded that only *some parts* of a given organizational culture have relevance to what the organization needs to do. As he discovered, Edgar Schein had been right all along that a change-oriented leader cannot produce change without metrics, but a measurement-oriented leader cannot produce change without a strategy that integrates the measurement into the fabric of the change process.

Through his research, Denison learned the importance of examining both *internal* factors and *external* forces. He and his team developed a way to measure culture—a way to count what counts—to help organizations focus on the issues that need attention and move beyond a discussion of employee satisfaction, engagement, and morale to better understand the decisions they must make to build organizations for the future and the actions leaders must take. He found successful organizations concentrate on their mission, adaptability, employee involvement, and consistency. When we zero in on the critical few and put aside the trivial many, we can act on an otherwise complex decision.

AGREE ABOUT THE RIGHT AND WRONG WAYS TO DO THINGS

The financial impact on hospitals in the aftermath of Hurricane Katrina varied depending on factors such as location, size, and resources available. While some hospitals faced *significant* financial challenges due to the destruction of infrastructure, loss of revenue from disrupted operations, and increased expenses associated with emergency response and recovery efforts, others were able to recover more quickly.

Agreeing about the right and wrong of post-Katrina decisions did not go smoothly, however. As often happens, dedication to their values often came at a significant financial cost as hospitals incurred expenses related to emergency response, infrastructure repairs, and uncompensated care. However, they prioritized the needs of their communities and demonstrated their commitment to their core values of *compassion, service*, and *equity,* even in the face of adversity.

In the *immediate* aftermath of the hurricane, many hospitals experienced financial strain as they grappled with the costs of rebuilding damaged facilities, replacing equipment, and providing care to a surge of patients. Additionally, disruptions to healthcare delivery systems and the displacement of populations served by these hospitals contributed to revenue losses.

However, over time, many hospitals recovered financially with the help of government aid, insurance payouts, and donations from individuals and organizations. Moreover, the increased attention on disaster preparedness and resilience in the healthcare sector following Hurricane Katrina helped hospitals strengthen their infrastructure and emergency response capabilities, which contributed to improved financial stability in the long term.

Ochsner Health System, based in New Orleans, serves as an example of how a hospital can regain financial security after a tragedy if leaders agree about priorities. Ochsner Health System, a nonprofit organization, faced significant challenges in the aftermath of the hurricane, including damage to facilities, displacement of staff and patients, and a surge in demand for healthcare services.

Despite these challenges, Ochsner Health System worked diligently to rebuild and restore its operations, leveraging various sources of financial support. The organization also implemented strategic initiatives to enhance its resilience and preparedness for *future* disasters.

Through its commitment to providing high-quality healthcare services to the community, Ochsner Health System eventually regained financial stability. Today, it is one of the largest healthcare providers in Louisiana, with multiple hospitals and clinics serving patients across the region. Ochsner Health System's successful recovery from Hurricane Katrina serves as a testament to its dedication to its mission and values, as well as its ability to adapt and thrive in the face of adversity.

Overall, while Hurricane Katrina had a significant financial impact on hospitals in the affected areas, many rebounded and continued providing essential healthcare services to their communities. Additionally, the lessons learned from this disaster have informed efforts to enhance resilience and preparedness in the healthcare sector to mitigate the impact of future crises.

NO MATTER WHO YOU ARE, DON'T IGNORE VALUES

Your organization needs to live its principles, not just write them. Your values should mean something and serve as criteria for making business decisions. Will you fire your company's most valued, high potential person for a violation of these values? What will you do to protect the environment? When you grapple with these kinds of questions, you will be able to develop a list of standards that will become more than a nice poster in your foyer; these values will serve as the bedrock of your strategy.

Twice Linda encountered situations when top performers lost their jobs because they ignored the organization's values. In the first instance, a stellar performer, Kevin, who served as a true rainmaker, didn't work well with others on the executive team. While conducting assessments of the team, she learned that at least two other stars on the team planned to leave unless the boss, Scott, did something to change the situation. In the interview, one man mentioned that he knew that Kevin had lied on his resumé.

Linda found Kevin impossible to work with, too. In fact, he walked out of his interview and had walked out of a meeting with his boss earlier that day, but when Linda gave Scott feedback about Kevin's behavior, Scott tried to dismiss it all until she mentioned that she suspected Kevin had lied on his resumé, and that Scott would need to notify corporate HR to discover whether he had. Kevin had alienated so many people along the way that HR was happy to investigate. Scott fired Kevin later the same day.

In another instance, the CEO of a small specialty hospital lost her job because she violated the rules concerning paid time off. Initially, as a highly valued leader of the hospital, she grew out-patient services, hired stellar physicians and nurses, and worked cohesively with the CMO to provide the best patient care in the region. But eventually she made no secret of the fact that she was seeing a married man and generally thought the rules didn't apply to her. She found out the hard way that the rules apply to everyone, especially someone whom the board doesn't respect because of the decisions she made in her personal life. She lost her job, and the hospital lost its most valuable employee.

REDUCE BUREAUCRACY

Organizational change, especially as it relates to cultural change, has dominated discussions since the 1980s. Theorists and practitioners argued *then* and disagree *now* about how to define it and how to measure it. Those disputes helped create the La Brea Tar Pit of good intentions.

For tens of thousands of years, oil seepage from the earth created craters of pitch in urban Los Angeles, known as the Le Brea Tar Pits. The tar formed a deposit thick enough to trap unsuspecting animals that wandered in, became trapped, and eventually died. Predators ventured in to eat the ensnared animals and found themselves stuck, too. Over many centuries, the Le Brea Tar Pits have trapped and preserved the remains of animals that once roamed the earth with pride and distinction—the victims of Mother Nature, other marauders, and their own bad judgment.

In the 20th Century people started using "culture" anthropologically to describe the range of human phenomena that cannot be attributed to genetic inheritance. It encompassed beliefs, customs, art, work, institutions, and use of symbols—the totality of socially transmitted behavior patterns. We understood the concept of "culture" as it related to the study and development of human societies.

Scholars, historians, and anthropologists traditionally shied away from *judgment* in their description of culture. They *depicted* the practices, policies, and patterns of a given people without adding editorial comment, often implying cultures aren't better or worse, just different. Well intended as this might have been, it was also wrong-minded and led to the formation of healthcare tar pits. Now we understand better that we need to make judgment calls—to *judge*, not just to *describe*—a hospital's culture.

This concept of culture and cultural change became important to leaders who wanted to understand the role *morale* and *corporate values* played in creating the environment of the company. Nearly everyone understood *then* and knows *now* that culture plays both a role in *constraining* change and in *causing* it. But few understood exactly *how* it played this role, and few agreed on what "it" was.

If we accept the definition that "it" is "the way we do things around here," we can also accede that some things never worked, and some things worked once but no longer work. Then it's time for an examination of how bureaucracy limits action. Changing the culture of a hospital involves these five steps:

1. Realization that things need to change
2. An answer to the question, "What do we want to be true a year from now that isn't true now?"
3. Metrics for assessing the change
4. A clear picture of the value of the change
5. Commitment to the needed changes

Kaiser Permanente changed its culture when leaders realized they needed to emphasize effective use of *electronic health records* and its proactive approach to patient care management, which helped in quickly translating insights into tangible health outcomes. Mayo Clinic encouraged a *collaborative environment* where a motivated staff pursues new ideas and approaches, making it a leader in medical excellence and transformative healthcare practices. Cleveland Clinic achieved numerous successes, such as developing *new treatments for complex medical conditions, reducing hospital readmissions*, and *improving patient outcomes* by concentrating on the value of the needed changes. Each of these three healthcare networks distinguished itself from others in different ways, but each achieved excellence through action, innovation, and change—not bureaucracy.

In a healthcare system, ineffective leadership seldom happens because of rusty management skills. Similarly, organizational disasters don't usually occur because of a flawed culture. No, poor leadership and corporate disasters happen when leaders persist in sloth-like approaches, ignoring the links among beliefs, decision-making, and results. Leaders need a new approach for thinking about the environment of the organization—a new ideology that inexorably links decision-making, action, and success.

CONCLUSION

The word "culture" has continued to morph as it describes organizational culture—the predominating attitudes and patterns of behavior that characterize a business. Some cultures work; others don't. Some succeed; some fail. Cultures don't merely differ. Those leaders who strive for anything other than excellence driven by integrity doom themselves and their organizations to stagnation and possible ruination.

At one time, ordinary services, management, and talent would have allowed you to stay in the game. Not anymore. Your patients and employees will reject your organization if you don't create a culture that nourishes their souls. If you count what counts, you'll run through the tape at the finish line and live to enter another race.

Section Two

Execution

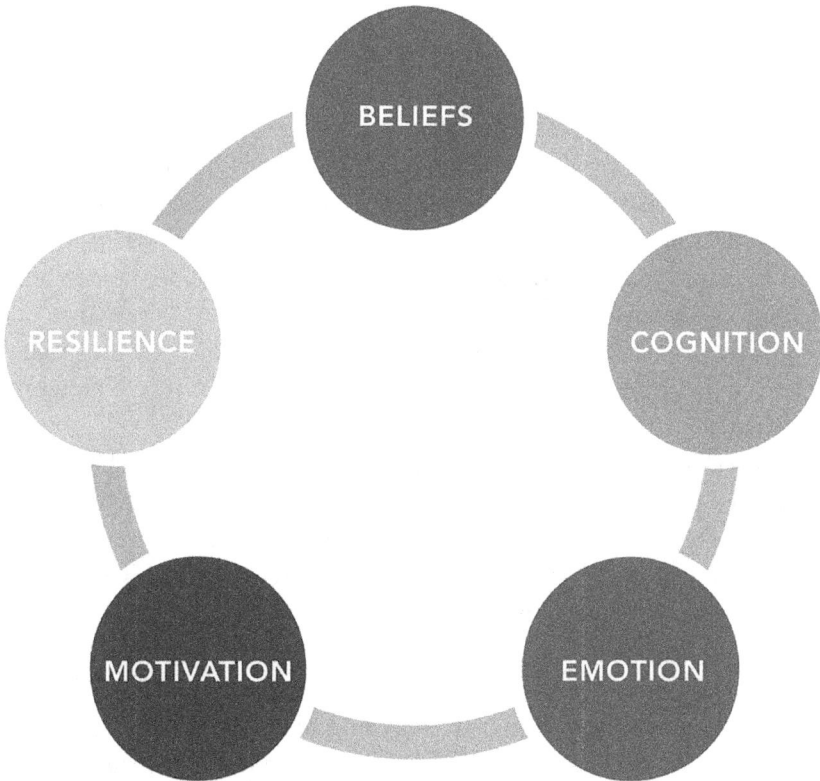

Why do some healthcare organizations hit the ground running, while others trip over their own shoelaces? The answer lies in the organizational DNA—the mindsets of executives: their values, cognitive skills, emotions, motivation, and resilience. Exceptional healthcare organizations serve as magnets to star performers who, by their very nature, require excellent performance of themselves and those with whom they associate. They want to feel empowered to make decisions to improve both the organization and their own lives, and they want to align their excellence with an employer that distinguishes itself through excellence.

These stars crave an action-oriented culture that responds to change and reinvents itself whenever new information or learning indicates it should. They want to work for organizations that strive to think strategically, grow dramatically, promote intelligently, and compete successfully—both today and tomorrow. That combination allows them to step to the front—to separate the duck from the quack and the ace from the pack. It allows them to deliver on a well-shaped strategy.

A breakthrough product, dazzling service, or cutting-edge technology can put you in the game, but only rock-solid *execution* of a well-developed strategy can keep you there. You must be able to deliver—to transform your brilliant strategy and operational decisions into *action*. If your organization is like many, however, in an effort to improve performance, too frequently you address the *symptoms* of dysfunction, not the root causes of it. You focus your attention and that of others on what's going wrong instead of *why* it doesn't work.

Done well, execution pushes you to translate your broad-brush theoretical understanding of the strategy into intimate familiarity with how it will work, who will take charge of it, how long it will take, how much it will cost, and how it will affect the organization overall. When you execute effectively, you get smart answers to these questions:

- How do we position ourselves against our competitors?
- How can we translate our strategy into *specific* results?
- How can we attract the right kinds of people to execute our plan?
- How do we make sure our activities deliver the outcomes to which we've committed?

In other words, the heart of execution lies in three core constructs: *a clear strategy, the right people, and efficient operations*. To implement the strategy successfully and get answers to the above questions, you'll need to address all three.

More organizations fail at execution than at strategy formulation. Corralling the executive team to spend a day or two hashing out the objectives for the year is the easy part. The hard work involves *implementing* ideas. As many leaders have observed, you're better off with a strategy that is 80% right and 100% implemented than with one that is 100% right but not fully executed.

Failure to link all elements of strategy to its execution explains why so many organizations crash in the implementation stage. If your mission is only a plaque in your foyer, your vision remains firmly planted in the CEO's head, and the strategy, if memory serves, somehow involved those two days the senior team spent at the resort shortly before the golf tournament, your organization might be on the road to perdition. Every healthcare organization is headed somewhere, but too often decision-makers don't consider all the elements of success when planning the path. Instead, executives engage in *reactive* decision-making or short-term gains designed to placate shareholders and analysts. The successful ones know they must do better.

Decentralization, rapid growth, and turmoil have become common in healthcare. Therefore, a corresponding need for protocols and procedures to ensure coherent strategic action has emerged. A new CEO may bring a new approach, but if the organization's mission remains the same, so does stability of execution. Strategy and execution portend success when they do these things:

- Force trade-offs among competing resource demands.
- Set clear boundaries within which decision-makers must operate as they experiment with innovative and traditional tactics.
- Seize opportunities.
- Eliminate bureaucracy.

Hiring well and giving yourself a talent advantage is the first step, doing everything to develop, retain, and leverage that talent the second. In organizations that can successfully implement their strategies, people know what decisions they can make and the criteria they should use for making them. They understand their responsibilities but also expect that, once they have been made, their decisions will not be second-guessed. They understand that with accountability comes the responsibility not just to deliver on objectives but also to make money in the process—an important element that many organizations fail to evaluate. Star performers know they must deliver results, but they insist on fair compensation when they do.

Creative thinking shapes strategy, but the hard work involves *implementing* ideas. The operating plan provides the *path* to do that. It breaks long-term strategic goals into short-term targets. Meeting those targets forces decisions that need to be integrated across the organization, both in response to internal and external business conditions.

You don't want your operating plan to concentrate on the past—to focus on the reflection in the rearview mirror. You also don't want it to be a distortion of future possibilities—like an image in a fun house mirror. Instead, your operating plan should be a kaleidoscope that exhibits various symmetrical patterns that reflect the loose bits of information you have aggregated. As you rotate it with new information and contingencies, new patterns and answers will appear. It is a look forward to "how's." It includes the programs your organization will complete within a year to reach your strategic objectives in four major areas: finance, customers, processes, and people. When you tie a culture of discipline to a commitment to attract and retain the best and brightest in your industry, a magical alchemy of action and results occurs.

Talent lies at the heart of all progress and productivity. Without it, nothing else matters. Instead of solving problems and repeatedly returning the organization to the status quo, your talent must innovate to formulate a successful strategy and then apply advanced critical thinking to develop the plan for execution. The formula may seem easy, but judging from the number of organizations that allow the strategy to die before it's executed (pun intended), it's not easy. Only a select few can sort out what needs to be done to turn great strategy into great execution.

4

Leverage Technology

Why do some healthcare organizations embrace change while others fail to do so? Why do some hospitals make disruption their goal with no clear objective for doing so? A goal to grow an organization will inevitably lead to disruption, but a goal to disrupt won't lead to growth. In fact, a goal to change for the sake of change will more likely lead to loss of market share, patient loyalty, and top performers. We look to research in psychology for answers.

In 2006, after decades of research, Stanford University psychologist Carol Dweck, Ph.D., introduced a simple but revolutionary idea: the power of mindset. Her research indicated that how we think about our talents and abilities determines our success in every human endeavor—school, work, sports, business—and even medicine. In her groundbreaking book, *Mindset: The New Psychology of Success*, Dweck noted that people with a *fixed mindset*—those who believe that abilities are permanent—flourish less often than those with a *growth mindset*—those who believe they can develop abilities.

Others since Dweck have introduced the terms "poverty mindset," and "scarcity mindset." Poverty mentality influences behaviors consistent with beliefs that money shouldn't be spent; we have limited opportunities; risk brings too much danger; success is temporary and non-replicable; and generally, remaining in the back of the pack is safest. This sort of scarcity mindset tells us there will *never* be enough, so we must steadfastly guard what we have.

Conversely, an "abundance mindset" assures us we can attain and replicate success. We will *always* have enough, so we can afford to take risks. We have the talent to handle most situations we encounter successfully.

DOI: 10.4324/9781003596912-6

(And in those times when we can't, we will be resilient enough to bounce back quickly.)

Dweck offered a simple but revolutionary view of achievement: how we see our intelligence, personality, and talent influences how we learn, work, live, love, and succeed or fail in life. She also exhibited what we call a *disruptive mindset*.

HAVE THE "DISRUPTIVE MINDSET" YOU WILL NEED TO CHANGE AND IMPROVE

In 2005, David Geary introduced *The Origin of Mind: Evolution of Brain, Cognition, and General Intelligence.* In this work, the author discussed Charles Darwin's opinion that understanding the evolution of the human mind and brain stands at the heart of evolutionary sciences. Geary drew from Darwin's observations to propose an integrated theory of why and how the human mind has developed to function as it does. He posited that human motivation, emotional, behavioral, and cognitive systems have evolved to process social and ecological information. He further argued that the ultimate focus of all these systems is to support our attempts to gain access *to* and control *of* resources—the social, biological, and physical resources that support survival.

Today most experts agree the conventional "nature or nurture" questions don't really help us understand human behavior. We now know that our genes and the environment cooperate as we develop. However, we also now understand that we have more capacity for lifelong learning and brain development than we previously imagined. More than 100 years ago, Alfred Binet, the French psychologist who developed the first practical IQ test, noted that the people who start out the smartest don't end up the smartest. To our knowledge, Binet never used the word "mindset," but his writing suggests he understood the concept a century ago.

When Linda and Dr. Constance Dierickx wrote *The Merger Mindset: How to Get It Right in the High-Stakes World of Mergers, Acquisitions, and Divestitures,* they concluded that *the view you adopt for yourself profoundly affects the way you lead your life—and how you engage in high-stakes decision-making.*

Drawing from Dr. Dweck's work, we explored how believing that a *fixed mindset*—one that tells us our talents and qualities resist change—creates an urgency to prove ourselves over and over. This kind of mindset erects roadblocks to our success and keeps us in a constant, confusing spiral. We see our gifts—or the lack thereof—as the hand we were dealt and must live with.

Conversely, a *growth mindset* causes us to believe that the hand we're dealt is just the starting point for development. We view our talents as attributes we can cultivate through our efforts and strategies. Although people may differ in every significant way—in their initial talents, aptitudes, and temperaments—everyone can change and grow through application and experience. Dweck asked, "Do people with this mindset believe that anyone can be anything, that anyone with proper motivation or education can become Einstein or Beethoven?" No, but they believe a person's true potential remains unknown (and unknowable) and that no one can foresee what an individual can accomplish with years of passion, toil, and training.

We once considered many of the people we now consider shining stars dull. High school coaches once cut professional athletes we now deem "great" from JV teams. Teachers once considered Darwin and Tolstoy ordinary children. Ben Hogan, one of the greatest golfers of all time, appeared completely uncoordinated and graceless as a child. Drama instructors routinely advised today's stars to give up on acting careers. However, these "greats" had a growth mindset that allowed them to overcome their weaknesses and ignore the wrong-headed advice of their coaches and critics. In other words, the people with the growth mindset were amazingly accurate, and those with a fixed mindset were wrong. An appetite for stretching oneself and sticking to it even, or *especially*, when the going gets tough is the hallmark of the growth mindset. Those with this kind of mindset position their organizations to embrace scary cutting-edge solutions.

INSIST ON A CUTTING-EDGE APPROACH TO TELEHEALTH

At the end of 2019, using the principles of the late management guru Peter Drucker, *The Wall Street Journal* announced its picks for the best-managed companies of the year. Of 820 companies, Amazon took first place, and Microsoft rose to the number two position, followed by Apple in third place—all companies that relied on cutting-edge technology. A team of researchers compiled the list using dozens of data points to evaluate companies on five performance dimensions: customer satisfaction, employee engagement and development, innovation, social responsibility, and financial strength—the same criteria we use to evaluate healthcare facilities.

The performance dimensions describe these top-ranking companies, but they do more. They give us a glimpse into the mindset decision-makers shared. That is, we can infer that senior leaders and board directors held some common beliefs about what success looks like and had the requisite talents, skills, and confidence to get the results they wanted.

We can also conclude that an unprecedented number of challenges continue to differentiate leaders who embody a disruptive mindset from their competitors who don't. At the same time, we can extrapolate that the way we have traditionally assessed an organization's ability to grow through innovation and transformation is outdated.

When Jeff Bezos founded Amazon, he didn't assemble retail experts to advise him about how to do something no one had done before. Taxi drivers didn't start Uber, and horse breeders didn't start the Ford Motor Company. Rather, these successful companies exist because of innovative solutions that *came from those with disruptive mindsets*.

Amazon catapulted to the top of the 2019 list by earning an off-the-chart ranking in *innovation*. Its score in that dimension of performance is more than double that of any other company. Amazon outpaces others in patent applications, trademark registrations, and spending on research and development. Amazon also *abandons* patent applications at a higher rate than others, a sign of its commitment to move past obsolete technology.

Bezos has long-shunned lengthy slide presentations. Instead, employees present a memo that may not be longer than six pages. Everyone reads it prior to starting a meeting. Bezos praised the memo process in one of his letters to investors: "Some have the clarity of angels singing." This succinct summary sets up the meeting for high-quality discussions, a fast pace, and agility—the opposite effect of cumbersome PowerPoint presentations in most other organizations.

Disruption alone doesn't create growth. Instead, *growth creates disruption*. Disruption for the sake of disruption would earn a low-ranking score among the companies the *Wall Street Journal* evaluated. For instance,

Facebook Inc. received a low score on customer satisfaction, a score based on customers' unwillingness to recommend Facebook to a colleague or friend. *Borat* star, Sacha Baron Cohen, attacked Mark Zuckerberg in a speech in November 2019 at the Anti-Defamation League's International Leadership Summit, saying the social media giant's resistance to fact-checking ads relies on "twisted logic" that would have had it selling spots to Nazis in another generation. Many would argue Facebook experienced its share of disruption in 2019, but that disruption led to a sullied reputation, not growth and admiration.

A disruptive mindset involves more than innovation, cutting-edge technology, pace, and risk-taking—but they help. Disruption can happen slowly and methodically, causing so little discomfort that few would choose the word "disruptive" to describe the transformation. More often, however, disruption shows up dragging a breathless sense of urgency—if not crisis—with it.

We think about all the changes we've seen since we started working in healthcare more than 40 years ago: X-ray film, once considered cutting-edge, has now largely been replaced by digital radiography. Many thought paper medical records, where Debbie got her start, were innovative when first systematized but now obsolete in favor of Electronic Health Records (EHRs). Digital and infrared thermometers have replaced mercury thermometers, once the standard. Cutting-edge in the 1980s and early 1990s, floppy disks have become completely archaic. Pagers for doctors, once groundbreaking for on-call communication, have given way to smartphones and secure messaging apps. Linda remembers the days of "Dr. Henman, please dial the operator." Mechanical ventilators, while still in use, are judged out-of-date compared to microprocessor-controlled ventilators.

When Constance Dierickx and Linda wrote *The Merger Mindset*, they built on Dweck's research but tailored the concept to apply to high-stakes decisions like the use of state-of-the art technology. They noticed that successful leaders who make the important decisions for an organization have five things in common: a strong belief in themselves, and the requisite intellectual horsepower, fortitude, motivation, and resilience. Decisions about technology require all five, too. Only then can the healthcare executives develop the Disruptive Mindset™ that will determine how to use facts to help them make the technological decisions that will take them into the next decade.

TAKE A FACT-BASED APPROACH TO DECISION-MAKING

When ambiguity shows up with adversity, they impose themselves without invitation. In these situations, we can link the willingness to *tolerate* ambiguity with the will to overcome adversity to begin a successful next chapter.

Decisiveness under pressure requires *high-ambiguity tolerance.* When people tolerate, or even appreciate ambiguity, they demonstrate the ability to *synthesize* facts. As we recall from chemistry classes, synthesis is the production of a substance from simpler materials after a chemical reaction. In healthcare organizations, executives must play the role of chemists to create the reaction they want for themselves and for those who depend on them.

We call executives who are decisive but who have a low tolerance for ambiguity *aggregators.* That is, they make decisions based on loosely associated fragments of information, but they lack the ability to *analyze* or *synthesize* it. This works under ordinary circumstances, but during times of change, especially unexpected, unwelcome changes, they'll find little that's ordinary.

The *analysts* don't fare so well amid disorder. Their tendency toward indecision, coupled with their intolerance of ambiguity, often explains why a decision or ill-advised choices create more problems. The *speed* of decision-making becomes more important in high-stakes, crisis situations, especially those involving cutting-edge technology and pioneering treatments.

Theorists, those who enjoy an element of ambiguity but who find decision-making daunting, won't do better. Given enough time, they can make the right call, but once again, opportunities appear and disappear quickly.

Decisive

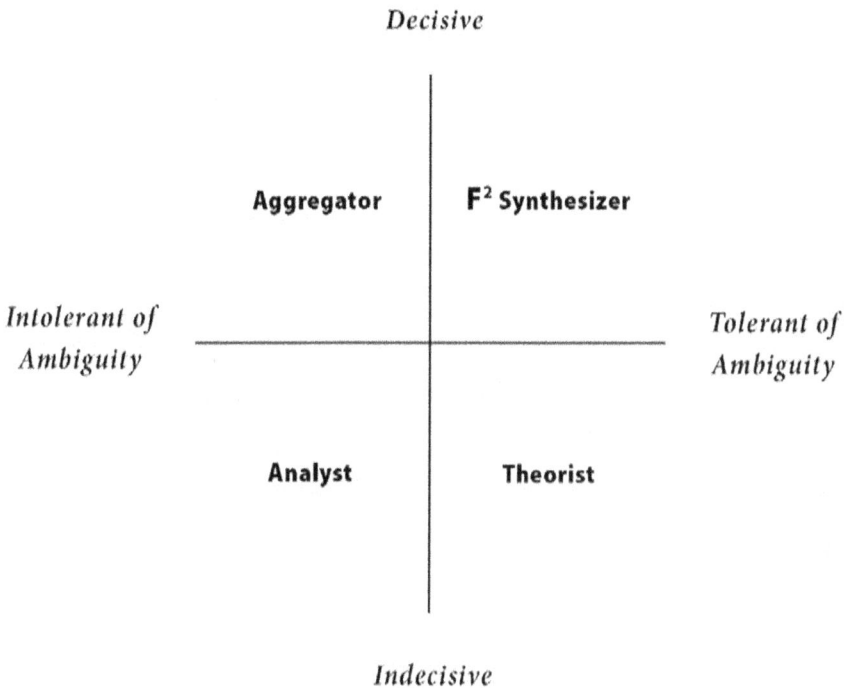

Aggregator	**F² Synthesizer**

Intolerant of Ambiguity ——————————|—————————— *Tolerant of Ambiguity*

Analyst	**Theorist**

Indecisive

We call those decisive executives who have a high tolerance for ambiguity F² Synthesizers, leaders who are both firm and fair. These decision-makers balance fairness and a concern for people with firmness and a concern for results.

F² executives at Massachusetts General Hospital (MGH) enjoy a strong reputation for their decisiveness, ambiguity tolerance, and general evidence-based approach to decision-making. They have a strong focus on research and use data to inform their clinical practices. For example, MGH implemented a data-driven system to monitor and prevent hospital-acquired infections, which led to significant reductions in infection rates.

At the same time, MGH demonstrated a willingness to embrace ambiguity and tackle complex challenges, as evidenced by its approach to the opioid epidemic. Recognizing the complexity of the issue, MGH launched a multidisciplinary program called the *Substance Use Disorders Initiative*. This initiative brings together experts from various fields to develop innovative solutions that address the medical, psychological, and social aspects of addiction.

Their response to the COVID-19 pandemic offers another example. In the face of a novel virus with many unknowns, MGH quickly adapted its operations and treatment protocols based on emerging evidence. They also participated in clinical trials and research efforts to better understand the virus and develop effective therapies, even as the situation continued to evolve.

By embracing ambiguity and taking a proactive approach to complex challenges, while still grounding their decisions in facts and evidence, MGH has demonstrated a balance between fact-based decision-making and the ability to navigate uncertainty. This approach has allowed them to remain at the forefront of medical care and research, while also responding effectively to emerging health crises.

MAKE SURE PHYSICIANS STAY UP TO DATE ON ELECTRONIC HEALTH RECORDS (EHRs) SYSTEMS

Electronic Health Record systems have been around for a long time. The Regenstrief Institute in Indianapolis, now known as the Sidney & Lois Eskenazi Hospital, developed the first EHR system in 1972, and about the same time, the VA developed the Veterans Health Information Systems and Technology Architecture (Vista). Gradually, other healthcare organizations established ways to gather and store information about patients, but incentives associated with The Health Information Widespread Technology for Economic and Clinical Health (HITECH) Act of 2009 changed things rapidly. Since then, most hospitals and physicians' offices in the United States have implemented EHRs, though the specific systems vary among institutions.

EHR systems leverage the power of data-driven approaches to improve patient care, streamline healthcare operations, and advance medical research. EHRs contain a wealth of information about patients' medical histories, treatments, medications, diagnoses, and outcomes. By using *machine learning*, healthcare professionals can also analyze vast amounts of data to identify trends, predict patient outcomes, personalize treatment plans, detect anomalies, and optimize healthcare processes.

Stanford Medicine has been at the forefront of applying machine-learning techniques to electronic health records to improve patient care, clinical decision-making, and healthcare outcomes.

By applying machine-learning algorithms, researchers at Stanford researchers have been able to discern *patterns* that have led to better decisions about how to improve overall care delivery, especially for high-risk patients.

Stanford Medicine and others have transformed healthcare delivery by enabling more personalized, data-driven, and efficient care, while also empowering researchers to make new discoveries and insights from the vast amounts of data contained within EHRs. Why then do many users resist using EHRs to their fullest potential?

Entering data into an EHR can be time-consuming, and physicians often feel pressure to see more patients in less time, leading to incomplete or rushed data entry, and some find navigating and entering the data difficult. Additionally, different EHR systems do not always communicate with each other seamlessly, creating more complexity.

Ambient listening technology in hospitals, a relatively recent development, has emerged and gained traction in the last five to ten years. These systems typically use *speech recognition* and natural language processing to automatically document patient-clinician conversations and capture important clinical information.

Some large healthcare systems and academic medical centers began piloting and adopting ambient listening between 2015 and 2017. As the technology matured and showed promise for reducing the administrative burden on clinicians, wider adoption occurred shortly after that. Beth Israel Deaconess Medical Center (BIDMC) in Boston began using ambient listening technology in 2020 as part of a pilot program to improve *physician documentation* and reduce the administrative burden on healthcare providers. From 2020 onward, the pandemic accelerated interest in ambient listening systems as healthcare providers sought ways to reduce physical contact and improve efficiency.

Ambient listening and other technological advancements continue to evolve because the rewards for staying up to date have become more obvious to decision-makers. Fragmentation and inconsistency put health providers at risk of having an incomplete or inaccurate overview of a patient's health history, thereby compromising quality patient care. It also means that health professionals often must manually re-enter data into multiple systems, leading to major inconsistencies or errors. By implementing *interoperability* standards—methodologies and technologies that allow different systems to share and exchange data easily—practitioners can synchronize online health records, gain full visibility across a patient's full scope of care, and make more informed patient care decisions.

Most of all, general resistance to change explains why some physicians, especially those who have been practicing for many years, resist adopting new technologies or changing their workflows; and some simply haven't had adequate training on new techniques, so they don't utilize the system's full capabilities. When physicians clearly see the links between using an EHR system effectively to improve patient outcomes *and* to advance better financial health for the organization, they can become both champions of and agents for necessary changes.

IMPROVE PATIENT CARE WITH ADVANCED TECHNOLOGY

Not all innovations in healthcare are related to advancements in technology, but most strategies and execution plans can trace their origins to a decision that involved a disruption of the status quo. For example, in 2020, Banner Health played a crucial role in managing the COVID-19 crisis in Arizona, one of the hardest-hit states in the United States. They rapidly expanded their telehealth services, allowing patients to receive care remotely, and it reduced the risk of exposure to everyone involved—patients, nurses, physicians, and technicians. This allowed patients to receive care from the comfort and safety of their homes and improved access to care for patients in rural areas or those with mobility issues. Then and now, Banner Health utilizes *remote monitoring technologies* to keep track of patients' vital signs and health status outside of the hospital setting. This enabled early intervention and reduced readmissions, leading to better patient outcomes. Banner Health also collaborated with the state government and other healthcare providers to set up *drive-through testing sites* and increase hospital capacity to handle the surge of COVID-19 patients.

As the Chinese proverb states, "The best time to plant a tree was 20 years ago. The next best time is now." Before the pandemic, Banner opened the *Banner Innovation Group in 2019*. This facility—one dedicated to developing and implementing new technologies and care delivery models to improve patient outcomes and reduce costs—led to their being recognized for their commitment to innovation and quality care. They weren't 20 years ahead of the others, but even one year gave them an edge over others in their responses.

Hospitals began exploring and gradually adopting AI technologies in the 1960s and 1970s, when early experimentation with AI in medicine began primarily in academic settings. In the next two decades after that, research continued, but technological constraints limited practical applications. By 2010, machine-learning algorithms for image analysis began to show promise in radiology. By the early 2020s, improvements in computing power and data storage made AI more viable in healthcare settings, and Electronic Health Records became more common, providing data for AI systems.

After that, AI dependence in hospitals began to increase rapidly with hospitals using it for predictive analytics, diagnostics, and administrative tasks. By 2020, the world had changed, and AI became part of that change. There's nothing like a pandemic to give technology a kick in the pants! Widespread dependence on AI gave hospitals that kick after COVID-19 started.

Regulations and best practices for AI use in healthcare continue to evolve, which affects the rate and extent of AI adoption in hospitals. As of this writing, AI has become increasingly integrated into many aspects of hospital operations and patient care. The following carried the torch of the early adopters:

Memorial Sloan Kettering Cancer Center (MSKCC), New York
MD Anderson Cancer Center, Texas
Cleveland Clinic, Ohio
Mayo Clinic, Minnesota
Massachusetts General Hospital and Brigham and Women's Hospital, Boston
Stanford Health Care, California
Johns Hopkins Hospital, Maryland
University of Pittsburgh Medical Center (UPMC), Pennsylvania:

We should recognize that many of these early adopters are large *academic medical centers* or *cancer-focused* institutions. Note the prevalence of names we've already cited in this book. These types of hospitals often have the resources and research focus to experiment with new technologies like AI. Also, "early adoption" can mean different things for different AI applications. Some hospitals might have been early adopters of AI for administrative tasks but later adopters for clinical applications, or vice versa. Smaller, more modestly funded hospitals can follow these vanguards and advocate for changes as quickly as their budgets will allow.

Although AI in healthcare has evolved rapidly, changing the landscape of adoption, implementation continues to change; and while AI has become more prevalent in healthcare, most hospitals are not yet fully "dependent" on it. Instead, providers typically use AI as a tool to augment and support *human* decision-making rather than replace it entirely. The integration of AI and other advanced technology into hospital systems is an ongoing process, with some institutions adopting these technologies more quickly than others. At all times, the focus should be on improving patient care, not just acquiring the latest and greatest bells and whistles.

WHAT THE FUTURE HOLDS

Advancements in technology costs will continue to come down, even as workforce expenses will rise. As the Baby Boomer nurses and doctors retire, hospitals will need to fund retirement plans as the *supply* of experienced healthcare providers decreases as demand for them rises. Skill sets of past decades will no longer be sufficient as higher demand for data analysts, health informaticians, specialized technicians, genetic counselors, and ethicists surges grows.

Actionability of the data collected will also remain a challenge. Actionability refers to how effectively healthcare providers, patients, or systems can use collected data to improve health outcomes, streamline processes, or make better clinical decisions.

However, the overall increase in information on outcomes and practice patterns, along with more effective dissemination of data, will enable faster and more accurate treatment decisions. Current struggles with *interoperability* will be overcome, and data will follow patients in a more efficient manner. Interoperability of data in a hospital setting refers to the ability of different information technology systems and software applications to communicate, exchange data, and use the information that has been exchanged.

Most, if not all, changes in the future will be tied to improvements in artificial intelligence. Artificial Intelligence and Machine Learning (AI and ML) are poised to revolutionize diagnostics that use machine-learning algorithms that can predict disease outbreaks, drug discovery and development, personalized treatment plans, and administrative processes. AI and MI will enhance early disease detection, improve treatment efficacy, and streamline healthcare operations. AI-assisted drug development will allow pharmaceutical companies to use predictive models to design and test potential drugs in a matter of days or weeks rather than the years it now takes.

Telemedicine and Remote Patient Monitoring during the COVID-19 pandemic accelerated the adoption of telemedicine. This trend will continue with more sophisticated remote monitoring tools, allowing for better management of chronic conditions and improved access to healthcare in underserved areas.

Advanced diagnostic capabilities will expand, too. Point-of-care devices and at-home testing kits will provide quick and accurate results for a wide range of conditions, enabling early detection and timely treatment.

The development of *lab-grown organs* for transplants will address the organ shortage crisis, eliminating waiting lists, reducing rejection risks, and improving transplant outcomes. In some cases, providers will enable personalized organ development using the patient's own cells.

Precision medicine and advancements in genomic sequencing and analysis will enable more personalized treatment plans based on an individual's genetic makeup. This will lead to more effective treatments with fewer side effects. Comprehensive genome sequencing will become a standard part of medical evaluations, providing insights into an individual's predisposition to diseases and guiding personalized treatment plans.

Clustered Regularly Interspaced Short Palindromic Repeats (CRISPR), a revolutionary gene-editing technology, holds immense potential for treating genetic disorders, developing new therapies, and potentially eradicating certain diseases. As they become more refined and widely accepted, they will transform the approach to many previously untreatable conditions.

As technology advances, so will concerns about its misuse. Critics have already expressed misgivings about altering the human gene pool with unpredictable long-term consequences. The creation of "designer babies" that only wealthy individuals and nations will be able to afford will further exacerbate existing social inequalities. Many fear the "playing God" element or fundamentally altering nature, thereby causing new health problems or genetic disorders. Of course, we will face supervisory challenges and government intervention when rapid advancements outpace regulatory frameworks.

In other words, in the next ten years, we will face the same kinds of challenges and opportunities we've always had. These controversies have led and will lead to ongoing debates in scientific, ethical, and policy circles about how to responsibly develop and use technology—and we predict they will continue to do so. Healthcare organizations need to start planting new trees now.

CONCLUSION

A disruptive mindset starts with a clear vision of what should change and what should stay the same. Any other approach will upset the ecosystem of the organization unnecessarily, unreasonably, and unwisely. How we think about our talents and abilities determines our success in every arena of human endeavor and separates the winners from the also-rans or the never tried. Hospitals that prioritize patient care will also be the ones that enjoy the financial rewards of doing so.

5

Adapt to Evolving Healthcare Needs

American author, organizational consultant, and expert on change and transitions, William Bridges, made a clear distinction between change (which is situational) and transition (which is psychological). He argued that it's not the change itself that people resist, but rather the transition. British author Richard Dawkins observed that yesterday's dangerous idea is "today's orthodoxy and tomorrow's cliché." Researcher James O'Toole addressed the emotional side of change when he wrote about "the ideology of comfort and the tyranny of custom," pointing out that a status quo mindset does more than create a philosophy; it establishes a risk-averse, oppressive dogma that quashes new ideas, novel approaches, and innovation. Each of these experts pointed out that organizational change, the double-edged sword, can build a technology giant like Apple, but it can also unleash a backlash of unrest and turbulence, depending on how executives lead others through the change.

Intellectually, healthcare executives understand they must champion change to keep pace with and outrun their competition. Yet, people often feel trapped by their own ideology, acting as though an oppressive regime or organizational structure has been forced on them by an unknown agent. They see themselves as victims. Usually, *they* have created their own traps and tyranny by making the status quo resistant to change. Imprisoned by their own behavior, they avoid conversations that would help them discover the gaps between their *intention* to change and their *decisions* to change.

Where does the balance between honoring the hospital's history and embracing the future occur? When does a stake in the ground serve as a sign of commitment, and when does it tether the warrior to his grave? We need to understand the rewards of change and the pitfalls of getting it

DOI: 10.4324/9781003596912-7

wrong. Only then can we address the tough calls leaders must make to serve as agents for and champions of change while preserving the best of what should *never* change. It all comes down to flexibility in decision-making.

MAKE THINGS FLEXIBLE AND EASY TO CHANGE

Flexibility describes the degree of organization in our lives and the extent to which we feel comfortable with *unstructured* and *unpredictable situations*, the ambiguity that surfaces most profoundly during times of change. Life is unpredictable, so our responses to the problems it creates need to be too. Mental agility has another important payoff: It stimulates *creativity*. Being open to a variety of creative and imaginative alternatives allows us to avoid getting trapped into thinking we have only one possible resolution. When you encourage your leadership team to avoid rigidity in their thinking, to experiment with innovation, and to seek the input of others, they can become more open to new ways of solving problems.

Once you help people quit fighting the currents and learn to flow *with* them, they can approach decision-making with new dexterity and energy. No one can control change, yet if we're not careful, it will control us, but usually change comes more from *imposition* and less from *invitation*. When people feel forced to adjust to new, uninvited changes, they feel out of control—a common, normal response.

Too often people think of change as a stellar opportunity to lose control of their lives, not as an exciting opportunity to improve them. They sacrifice themselves on the altar of custom when they imagine change in broad, sweeping terms and allow their fears to tyrannize them. When these fears surface, a wrong-headed approach to innovation permeates the organization like cancer. Many executives take a different approach. They walk toward change as Gladiators walking into an arena, hearing the crowd chanting their names. But successful healthcare executives eventually learn that drastic change seldom works as well as *steady, incremental* change.

These organizational gladiators also never underestimate the value of the short-term win. They know real transformation takes time, and without the small victories along the way, people lose their focus and sense of urgency, which leads to feelings of defeat.

Our most successful clients don't allow their competitors to define the playing field. Instead, they challenge themselves to see opportunities their competitors don't see. They redefine the terms of competition by embracing one-of-a-kind ideas in a world of copy-cat thinking. They look two years out and ask what will be different—both the challenges and the opportunities. They then ask the important question: How can we position ourselves to be ready for that new playing field?

One of our most successful clients asked that question recently. In a world where the lowest bid usually lands the deal, leaders at this organization realized they needed novel ways to distinguish themselves from the competition—new ways to stand out. They accomplished this goal by researching new financing options for their clients, making it easier to get money for the project, which made it easier to do business with our client. The same client realized they couldn't be merely "pretty good" at everything anymore; they had to become the *best* at something, so they improved their hiring processes to hire strong decision-makers who could more readily and effectively solve problems that didn't exist before.

Eventually, every successful organization must determine how to become the best at something: the best value for the money, the best at customer service, or the best quality. Healthcare organizations used to feel comfortable in the middle of the road—that's where all the patients were. Today, the middle of the road is the road to ruin. You must distinguish yourself in some way, and you can't be all things to all people.

When we help healthcare organizations with strategy or change initiatives, we begin by asking, "If your organization went out of business tomorrow, who would miss you and why?" The answer frames the discussion about what small changes will ensure the hospitals retain existing patients while it looks at changes to bring new ones in the door.

Your unique contribution to the world defines the ways you must be alert to opportunities to change: "What technology/changes to process/services/intellectual property will we need to add? What steps must we take to retain our unique edge?"

The most creative executives we've worked with don't disavow the past. They apply previous learning and experience to new situations. They see patterns, so they know what to keep and what to discard meaning they don't advocate change for its own sake. Rather, they rediscover and reinterpret what must come before to ignite and foster innovation.

They also learn quickly. They realize they must keep pace with the rate at which the world changes. In a world that never stops changing, great leaders must never stop learning. How do you push yourself as an individual to keep growing and evolving—so your hospital can do the same? How can you commit to discovering the small—often daily changes that have the most profound results? Often the answer lies in looking back at what has defined success for the hospital up until now. Nothing fuels energy and succeeds like deconstructing success. When people take the time to examine what they've done and why it worked, they learn what they need to do *next* time—even though the same situation won't show up in the same way.

REACT WELL TO COMPETITORS' CHANGES AND OTHER CHANGES IN HEALTHCARE

We remember from our accounting classes that if we invest a dollar at 1% interest, in 72 days we'll double our money. The same applies to business. If we invest the time and resources to make *small 1% daily changes*, in a short time, we will compound interest (pun intended). It all starts with identifying both the strategic and tactical small changes that will have big results, which is what Kaiser Permanente did.

In the mid-2000s, traditional health insurance companies (UnitedHealth Group, Anthem, Aetna, among others) started offering a wide range of insurance products and expanding their networks. *Population Health Management*, a concept that emerged in the late 1990s and early 2000s, became more prominent in 2010 with the passage of the *Affordable Care Act*, which emphasized value-based care and preventative care. Kaiser Permanente gradually increased its investments and capabilities over time, and as an early adopter, soon outran its competitors.

About the same time, large hospital systems like Ascension Health, which was formed in 1999 through the merger of the Daughters of Charity National Health System and Sisters of St. Joseph Health System, started expanding its reach. By the early 2000s, Ascension had begun gradually acquiring or merging with other Catholic health systems and hospitals across the United States. This attracted more patients and increased their bargaining power with insurers. In response, Kaiser Permanente reacted by expanding into new markets and forming strategic partnerships.

Walgreens' retail clinic initiative started in 2005 with the Take Care Health Systems partnership. A year later, CVS acquired MinuteClinic, which integrated the clinic concept into CVS's retail pharmacy business. These clinics offered convenient, low-cost primary care services, drawing patients away from traditional healthcare providers. Reacting to the formation of these clinics, Kaiser Permanente put more focus on improving access to care and enhancing the overall patient experience.

Teladoc, an early entrant in the telemedicine field, began offering its services to a limited number of clients in 2005, marking the start of its commercial operations. In 2009, American Well partnered with Blue Cross Blue Shield of Hawaii to offer online care services. Both companies offered remote healthcare services, challenging the traditional in-person care model that Kaiser Permanente had been using. To compete with telemedicine providers and tech companies, Kaiser Permanente significantly expanded its telehealth services and digital health tools, which included partnering with tech companies.

To answer the shift toward value-based care models promoted by both competitors and government initiatives, Kaiser Permanente doubled down on its integrated care model and preventive health strategies. Kaiser Permanente's strategic moves addressed *specific* actions that countered the challenges posed by various competitors in the healthcare market, allowing it to maintain its market position and continue to grow in a rapidly evolving industry. These examples explain Kaiser Permanente's success in having its finger on the pulse of competitors' winning moves, but it doesn't clarify what executives need to do to *predict* changes.

They also became adept at spotting black swans. A "black swan" event, a term popularized by Nassim Nicholas Taleb, refers to an *unpredictable* event that is beyond what is normally expected of a situation and has potentially severe consequences. In healthcare, a recent notable example of a black swan event would be the emergence and rapid global spread of COVID-19 in 2019–2020. The pandemic reshaped many aspects of healthcare globally and continues to influence health policy, research priorities, and preparedness planning.

Preparing for black swan events presents a challenge, as these events are inherently unpredictable. However, leaders can take several steps to increase resilience and adaptability in the face of such occurrences. The strategies range from cultivating a culture of adaptability and developing robust risk management frameworks to investing in scenario planning and building strong networks. It also emphasizes the importance of financial flexibility, organizational agility, and continuous learning. These five decisions helped Kaiser Permanente prepare and respond to the black swan nature of COVID:

1. Kaiser had existing plans for pandemic scenarios, which provided a foundation for their response.
2. Their model of combining health insurance with healthcare delivery allowed for more coordinated responses.
3. Kaiser had already invested heavily in telehealth capabilities before the pandemic, which proved crucial.
4. They had systems in place for managing medical supplies, though these were strained during the pandemic.
5. Kaiser's robust data systems helped in tracking and responding to the spread of the virus.

Competitors' winning moves should trigger a response in healthcare executives, but so should black swan events because they can quickly reshape healthcare globally, influence health policy, research priorities, financial stability, and preparedness planning.

Proactively Embrace Innovation

In 2008, The Mayo Clinic established its Center for Innovation (CFI), which focuses on transforming healthcare delivery using *human-centered design approaches*, thereby establishing itself as a leader in healthcare innovation. Their timing was perfect. The late 2000s saw an increased focus on both patient-centered care and the need for change in the face of rising costs and shifting patient expectations. Mayo Clinic found itself at the forefront of a growing trend in healthcare to apply *design thinking*.

Design thinking focuses on understanding the needs, preferences, and experiences of patients, families, and healthcare providers. It requires *interdisciplinary collaboration* that often entails bringing together *diverse teams* of clinicians, researchers, and engineers to solve complex problems. *Ideation*, which plays a critical stage in design thinking, involves participants actively producing a wide range of ideas that lead to solutions.

Design thinking can be used to improve patient experiences, streamline clinical workflows, develop new healthcare services, technology—and just about anything else that needs a different approach. It encourages all the players to look at challenges from different perspectives, to uncover novel solutions to new problems and to address the old problems that just won't go away. When design thinking becomes part of a broader culture of unremitting improvement, decision-makers continue on a path that doesn't include backsliding.

The phrase "crossing the Rubicon" refers to any individual or group committing itself irrevocably to a risky or revolutionary course of action—the point of no return. In healthcare organizations, crossing the Rubicon need not involve treason or even revolutionary behavior. Rather, it means making the decision to innovate, to depart *radically* from the status quo, or to take the risks you've been avoiding.

So why, once the "die has been cast," do change initiatives still fail? Our experience has taught us that change usually fails for one of ten reasons:

1. Most people in most organizations can't recite the company's mission statement, much less articulate an ideal future state for the organization, so they don't understand *why* a change should happen.
2. Leaders show a reluctance to make the tough calls that the change needs to happen and will happen. They spend too much time "vetting" the decision in a feeble attempt to get buy in. Too much deliberation usually just frustrates people and delays the needed change.
3. Leaders lose sight of the macro, concentrating too much on the micro—too much focus on *tactics* and activities and not enough on *long-range goals.*
4. Leaders fail to serve as champions of or agents for the change, communicating that they will comply, rather than commit, to the change. We advocate robust debate about major changes to an organization, if those debates take place behind closed doors.
5. Too many people have an exaggerated concern about the disruptions that may happen in the short run instead of optimism about future gains and rewards.
6. People develop a propensity to fix current symptoms (to problem solve), which only restores circumstances to the status quo, ignoring innovative decision-making.
7. The focus turns inward, and people take their eyes off the patient.

8. Leaders hesitate or fail to delegate specific areas of the change initiative to individuals and withhold the authority and responsibility it would take to make the requisite decisions.
9. Leaders fail to hold people accountable for results.
10. Executives have a misguided notion that they know what will happen in 5 years, which can build either a false sense of security or a sense of dread among employees.

BREAK DOWN SILOS

The simplest explanation for why people resist change is that they fear more danger than opportunity. They see the change as unwanted, unknown, and unnecessary. Usually change involves loss, even if all they lose is predictability or familiarity. Change often creates emotional overload and chaos, two of the most potent ingredients in the recipe for resistance. We oppose change when we don't have confidence it will work, when we feel threatened, when we have no input in the decision, or when we just like things the way they were.

Individuals who violently oppose change can create culture traps to contain, compromise, or control it. However, when people work together to solve problems, they tend to have less fear of being blamed for a bad outcome, so they will advocate bolder actions because they will share the pain of a bad decision, even though they abdicate the glory of being the hero.

Why do people engage in behaviors that are counterproductive to their own stated objectives? Why do they deny they do that? And why do they deny they are denying? Fear causes people to develop the "victim mentality" to which we referred earlier. They begin to feel helpless—and the emotion can take on epidemic proportions. Soon, you'll find these people showing an unwillingness to face conflict and unpleasant situations because they fear even more loss. At all costs, they want to avoid threatening and embarrassing situations.

You'll find ego involvement with the status quo often prevents us from making changes we know will work. We look back and attempt to justify the decisions that created the status quo instead of examining *new* evidence that might cause us to change our minds. We lie to ourselves and others, saying what we decided *then* was the only thing that could have been done. This sort of self-fueling defense mechanism convinces us that our action represented a brilliant solution at the time. From that, we build defensive arguments that we should keep things as they are *now*.

Self-justification stands at the heart of cognitive dissonance—the mental stress of those who hold contradictory beliefs at the same time or who act in discord with their own beliefs. In his book, *Organizational Traps*, Chris Argyris called this the engine that drives self-justification, the mental discomfort people experience when others question their reason and falsify their predictions. We humans strive for consistency and abhor dissonance, so we take steps to ensure the former and eliminate the latter. This can lead to Machiavellian—the end justifies the means—actions that cause us to avoid any information that might inflict further discomfort. During times of change, successful leaders recognize they must comfort the afflicted and afflict the comfortable, but this requires herculean self-awareness, discipline, and restraint.

Others don't make the changes they know will work simply because they have a strong risk aversion. They don't like to gamble and want definitive, objective evidence that no part of the change can fail. Few change initiatives offer this sort of guarantee. When these people can't find the 100% reassurance they desire, they develop pessimism and question whether they ever believed the change would work. They also lack fortitude but try to mask this fact by claiming the need for more analysis.

The sort of pessimism that surfaces during planned change takes on the characteristic of a poverty mindset. Instead of recognizing that they have everything they need to make the changes, they doubt they will ever have enough—enough data, enough resources, enough control, enough talent, or enough strength—to make the tough calls, even when deep down they know they *can*.

Doing what you know will work requires all the constructs of tough calls—experience, moral gyroscope, judgment, and fortitude, but it demands more. Our moral gyroscope must compel us to *demonstrate* our integrity. We do not create integrity in a time of change or crisis, but we do reveal it. When we do, we not only know what will work; we do something with the knowledge, and we build cohesion in the process.

REWARD INNOVATIVE THINKING

Centuries ago, a two-part, seemingly contradictory pictogram from the Chinese language indicated an understanding of why people resist change. The bottom part of the symbol meant "opportunity"; the top character meant "danger." To the ancient Chinese, change included part danger, part opportunity. (Caesar probably would have agreed.) This ancient symbol helps explain why people have long resisted change or have become immobilized by it: They fear change will bring more danger than opportunity. The Chinese knew this centuries ago, and 21st Century leaders realize it every day. People don't really fear the change *itself*; rather, they fear the loss it might bring. Children don't fear the dark; they fear what might lurk in the dark. Employees don't differ.

Change, or transition, involves *movement*, a process that occurs in a series of steps. Sometimes change happens instantly, and the steps happen almost simultaneously, as they do during a crisis. But more often, change occurs over time and involves a transition from one state to another—a predictable process that occurs as people go through the stages of change, as they do in with a succession plan.

Researchers and theorists have defined these predictable stages. Kurt Lewin described three phases: unfreezing, movement, and refreezing. Linda's research with the Vietnam POWs indicated they went through three major stages that she calls Awareness, Adjustment, and Readiness to move forward. Typically, we go through these same three stages when a change occurs in our lives, regardless of the change. If we adapt, choose to go through the stages in a purposeful way, and earn the rewards of mastering the challenges of change presents, the three stages become our steppingstones to success and empower us to move toward triumph (Figure 5.1).

Just as we can learn to empower ourselves and move toward success, we can also learn helplessness. Angry or resistant, we imagine ourselves victims of change. We get stuck in one of the stages, and the stages become a progression that leads away from happiness. Leaders who want to keep the best and brightest people engaged can benefit from understanding these stages change so they can help those in their chains of command triumph.

When change comes into our lives, we can react in one of two ways: We resist, or we adapt. Similarly, when leading others, you can help them with

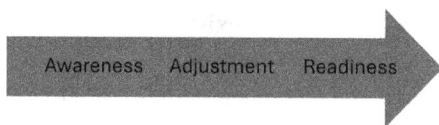

Awareness   Adjustment   Readiness

FIGURE 5.1

their reactions to change by managing your own responses more success-fully. Often you won't initially champion a change that circumstances or people have imposed on you. You might feel angry; you may be scared; you might even feel immobilized. But whatever your initial emotions, if you can put them aside, you will be better able to help others with their own feelings. This control occurs only when you better understand the change and when you go through this stage with a sense of clear-eyed optimism instead of head-down denial.

CONCLUSION

John Steinbeck said, "Change comes like a little wind that ruffles the curtains at dawn, and it comes like the stealthy perfume of wildflowers hidden in the grass." Change may come to authors like that, but in most hospitals, the change is more like a tornado than a gentle wind. Demands of the marketplace, the accelerating pace of globalization, innovative tech-nology, and new alliances—all have created needs for leaders to help their people respond quickly and repeatedly to change.

Some people thrive on change; they have trouble when things become too predictable or mundane. Those individuals will need your ideas for developing and challenging their talent. However, this chapter addresses the change-averse or change-challenged. This not-so-silent majority would prefer a root canal to any change in their software. To help them, therefore, you'll need to understand how to manage change and its impact on people—some of the most fundamental aspects of leadership.

The rapidity of change and the multi-faceted nature of it have created situations for which most of today's leaders have not prepared. The popu-lar leadership models that for so long provided formulae that equipped leaders to solve business problems have been inadequate and insufficient in today's world because the great thinkers who tested them did so in an age of slower change that no longer exists. Today the orthodoxies of main-stream change endeavors may not be enough to keep your people productive and engaged when they didn't welcome the change. Yet, despite the daunting complexities and uncertainties, we ask leaders to be the heroes and dynamic geniuses that will keep the doors open and the till full.

Managing change is a demand of leaders, the avoidance of it its antithesis. For centuries people have understood that the ability to know when to take risks, revolutionize, respond, and adjust separated those who succeeded from those who did not. Hundreds of years ago, Dante provided a warning to the leader who might be tempted to think otherwise. He described hell as "the miserable way taken by the sorry souls of those who lived without disgrace or without praise." Unlike hell, however, risk, change aversion, and the mediocrity that both often engender will not last an eternity. Those leaders who do not adjust and adapt both themselves and their organizations will quickly leave the competitive arena. Successful executives will take their places.

6

Prioritize Patient-Centered Decisions

In the ever-evolving landscape of healthcare, the cornerstone of exceptional patient care lies in the delicate balance of knowing patients, demonstrating unwavering commitment to their well-being, and fostering open communication. Healthcare providers who take the time to *understand* their patients' unique needs, preferences, values, and backgrounds lay the foundation for personalized, compassionate care and put their missions into action by steadfastly committing to *delivering* the highest quality of care.

As always, improvement in patient care starts with decisions at the top of the organization. When healthcare executives improve communication with physicians and nurses, they set the tone for everyone to be more in tune with what patients want and need. Decisions at the top provide the voice of improvement, the decisions everywhere else, the echo. When patients receive a clear, consistent message that their voices are joining the conversation, things change. A synergy occurs—one that leads to *reduced healthcare costs, increased patient loyalty, improved staff morale, and better compliance*—all constructs of a hospital with a clear strategy to grow and improve.

Implementing patient-centered care requires both tangible and intangible commitments from leadership, ongoing staff training, and a willingness to engage patients and families as active partners in the healthcare process. However, the benefits of patient-centered care make it a worthwhile investment for hospitals seeking to improve the quality, efficiency, and experience of healthcare delivery. It all starts with reliable date.

DOI: 10.4324/9781003596912-8

MAKE IT EASY FOR PATIENTS TO COMMUNICATE WITH YOU

When it comes to providers talking to their patients, talk is cheap, chiefly because supply exceeds demand. Usually, patients need you to *listen* to them more than you talk to them. However, that doesn't imply that you shouldn't be as committed to effective message *sending* as you are to successful message receiving. Therefore, striking a balance between communication overload and underload is an essential skill everyone needs to hone.

The success of communication relies heavily on the participants following certain unwritten rules so the receiver *decodes* the message in much the same way as the provider *encoded* it. Only then does effective communication occur. As simple as this process sounds, how often have you said something that you thought was perfectly clear, only to find out later that the receiver had taken it in *exactly* the wrong way?

For example, Linda's daughter ended up in the ER with a fever of an unknown origin. After exhaustive tests, the physician, who didn't speak English as a first language, attempted to explain that he had narrowed the possibilities to three things: a veerus (virus), inflammation of the gallbladder, or prostate problems. Sherry asked, "Do you really think I have prostate problems?" The annoyed physician attempting to explain himself responded, "You don't have a prostate, but I do think you have CMV, which stands for cytomegalovirus," which explained nothing.

Communication is a complex interaction, primarily because humans are involved; therefore, the provider's ability to communicate well with patients depends on three key factors: the proficiency to use language successfully, the skill to send congruent verbal and nonverbal messages, and the ability to listen to what's being said and what's *not* being said. When you've mastered these, you have a fighting chance that clear communication will occur, but even then, you can run into problems.

Problem One: Words Don't Mean; People Mean. Verbal communication involves the creation of meaning between people using words, the tools we need to transmit meaning from one person to the other. Words give us the ability to represent the world through symbols, a skill that allows us to make sense of our world and then to share that meaning with others. Our choice of words helps to shape our reality, and our perception of reality influences our choice of words.

The very words that empower us to create meaning with one another, however, can also create barriers between us because each of us assigns words the meaning we want them to have. The word *itself* doesn't have a universal meaning, even though millions of pages of dictionaries exist for the sole purpose of helping us develop common reactions to words. Instead, words serve as our code for transmitting our ideas and beliefs to others. The trouble is words, those pesky little rascals, can be used in more than one way. Intentionally or unintentionally, words can cause roadblocks to clarity.

For example, in an experiment conducted in Britain, people around the world were invited to judge jokes on an Internet site as well as contribute their own. The LaughLab research, carried out by psychologist Dr. Richard Wiseman, from the University of Hertfordshire, attracted more than 40,000 jokes and almost 2 million ratings. The following joke took first prize:

> Two hunters are out in the woods when one of them collapses. He doesn't seem to be breathing, and his eyes are glazed. The other guy takes out his phone and calls the emergency services.
>
> He gasps: "My friend is dead! What can I do?" The operator says: "Calm down, I can help. First, let's make sure he's dead."
>
> There is silence, then a gunshot. Back on the phone, the guy asks: "OK, now what?"

Sometimes the receiver decoding words differently than the sender intended is grist for the humor mill, but these mistakes don't serve us well when we try to send a message in earnest. In healthcare, we usually don't want others to view our words as jokes.

Words give us the means for sharing ideas and expressing emotion, but they can also serve as blockades. Certainly, the hunter and the emergency service operator experienced an impediment to effective communication. One of the reasons for these barriers is, even though meaning is not in words, we act as though it is. Just because a thought makes perfect sense in our heads doesn't in any way imply that anyone else will understand that idea in *exactly* the same way that we do.

Words are arbitrary mixtures of letters that represent concepts. Because concepts differ, and because people assign symbols to concepts in different and often unpredictable ways, misunderstandings occur. There are no guarantees that communication will ever occur in the way we intend for it to, but there are some things providers can do to try to control the direction a conversation goes, and hopefully avoid the fate of the hunter's friend.

A provider, therefore, should either speak the language of the patient fluently or invite someone who does into the conversation. When one of Linda's other daughters went into labor with her first baby, she lived in Sweden. The midwife attending her, who spoke perfect English, suggested that Laura use this opportunity to practice her Swedish (the exact opposite of patient-centered care). Laura replied between contractions that "I DON'T WANT TO PRACTICE MY SWEDISH!" which was a good call because she spoke very little Swedish.

Some nursing schools now require their graduates to demonstrate proficiency in Spanish, which makes perfect sense, especially for states bordering Mexico. One young woman in California said she would choose a nursing school that didn't require her to speak Spanish because she didn't agree with the "Spanishization of America," demonstrating the opposite of patient-centered care. (She never went to any nursing school, which probably worked out as it should have.)

Effective communication between healthcare professionals enables patients to actively participate in their own care and express concerns. Furthermore, accurate information about their health status, treatment options, and potential outcomes allows patients and their family members to make informed decisions. Patient feedback serves as a valuable tool for driving change and improvement within healthcare organizations, allowing them to identify areas of excellence and address any shortcomings in the patient's experience. By prioritizing these key aspects of patient care, healthcare providers create an environment that promotes healing, trust, and optimal health outcomes. That's what Dr. Slavin did.

Because the former president of Massachusetts General Hospital (MGH) in Boston, Dr. Peter Slaving, wanted to make it easier for everyone to reach him, he implemented a program called "Ask Allan," which provided patients and their families a direct line to communicate with him. The "Ask Allan" program allowed patients and families to send emails directly to Dr. Slavin with questions, concerns, or feedback about their experiences.

Dr. Slavin personally read and responded to each message, often within 24 hours. He also shared the feedback with relevant hospital leaders and departments to address problems and improve the patient experience.

When he demonstrated his commitment to patient-centered care and responsiveness to patient concerns, is it any wonder that his efforts led to increased patient satisfaction, trust in the hospital, and a positive impact on staff morale?

When healthcare executives tailor care to individual patient's needs, preferences, and values, it leads to better health outcomes. Because patient-centered care prioritizes communication, empathy, and respect, patients feel more involved and engaged in their care. Patients who feel heard are more likely to adhere to treatment plans and experience fewer complications, all leading to higher patient satisfaction and referrals.

KNOW WHAT YOUR PATIENTS WANT AND NEED

Hospitals that make patient-centered care a priority tend to have higher satisfaction scores because it drives *all* clinical decisions. This model of care recognizes patients as *unique* individuals with their own perspectives on health and well-being rather than passive recipients of medical treatment. Therefore, when healthcare providers actively listen to patients and involve them in decision-making processes regarding their care, providers can make better decisions.

Executives at Cullman Regional Medical Center Alabama took the time to find out what *their* patients wanted and needed; it all started with clear communication.

In 2016, Cullman Regional partnered with Philips Healthcare to conduct a comprehensive study to understand better the needs and preferences of their patients. They used a combination of *surveys, interviews,* and *focus groups* to gather feedback from patients, families, and staff members. Through this process, they identified several key areas for improvement, including these:

1. Enhancing communication between patients and care providers
2. Improving the overall patient experience
3. Streamlining the admission and discharge processes
4. Providing more personalized care and attention

Based on these findings, executives at Cullman Regional implemented several changes, including introducing a new patient engagement platform to facilitate better communication, redesigning patient rooms, and offering more flexible visiting hours. Almost immediately, Cullman saw *measurable* improvements in several key areas.

After the implementation of the patient-centered initiatives, Cullman Regional's patient satisfaction scores increased from the 28th percentile to the 98th percentile nationally, and the hospital's readmission rates decreased by 15% within the first year of implementing the changes, drastically improving quality scores, and demonstrating better patient outcomes and post-discharge care.

The average wait time in the emergency department decreased by 50%, from more than 100 minutes to less than 50 minutes. Cullman Regional Hospital Consumer Assessment of Healthcare Providers and Systems (HCAHPS) scores, which measure patient perceptions of their hospital experience, improved significantly in areas such as nurse communication, doctor communication, and overall hospital rating. The hospital also saw a 20% increase in employee engagement scores, suggesting the patient-centered approach had a positive impact on staff morale and satisfaction. These quantitative measures demonstrate the *tangible* benefits to a hospital that commits to patient-centered healthcare, but we shouldn't underestimate the value of the *intangibles* either. Patients want to *see* evidence, but they also want to *perceive* improvements.

COMMIT TO PATIENT-CENTERED HEALTHCARE

Patient-centered care requires seamless communication and collaboration among various healthcare providers. But it costs money before it starts saving money, and it has to start with a commitment from the CEO who looks for ways to provide better pain management and a comfortable environment for healing—two of the cornerstones of patient-centered healthcare.

Tailoring pain management strategies to individual needs, preferences, and medical histories empowers them and improves *treatment adherence* because pain management considers not just physical symptoms but also the emotional, psychological, and social impacts of pain. Additionally, proper pain management can lead to faster recovery, reduced hospital stays, and better overall health outcomes.

In 2019 the Cleveland Clinic made such a commitment to a comprehensive pain management improvement program called the "Opioid Stewardship Initiative." This initiative intended to improve pain management while reducing opioid use and associated risks, and they did. They accomplished these goals by doing the following:

- Using standardized pain assessment tools to ensure consistent evaluation of patient pain levels.
- Introduced multimodal pain management strategies for surgical patients, reducing opioid use.
- Incorporated Drug Monitoring Program (PDMP) checks into the electronic health record system to identify potential opioid misuse.
- Conducted extensive training on pain management best practices and opioid prescribing guidelines.
- Developed materials to inform patients about pain management options and opioid risks.
- Expanded access to non-pharmacological pain management options like acupuncture, physical therapy, and cognitive behavioral therapy.

By 2021, the Cleveland Clinic had achieved tangible, measurable outcomes. They had a 30% reduction in opioid prescriptions, decreased rates of opioid-related adverse effects, and improved patient satisfaction scores.

The University of Pittsburgh Medical Center (UPMC) also made a significant commitment to patient-centered care, but they took a different path. UPMC, a large, integrated healthcare system based in Pittsburgh, Pennsylvania, includes a network of hospitals, clinics, and other healthcare facilities. They established *Patient and Family Advisory Councils*, which work collaboratively with hospital staff to enhance the patient experience.

UPMC then introduced MyUPMC patient portals that allow patients to access their medical records, communicate with their healthcare providers, schedule appointments, and manage their health information securely. Many other healthcare systems implemented such portals in the early 2020s as part of the push toward electronic health records and patient engagement. UPMC Shadyside Hospital showed its commitment to patient-centered care when it renovated patient rooms to include features such as private bathrooms, adjustable lighting, and comfortable seating for family members.

UPMC's commitment to patient-centered care led to several quantifiable improvements in patient satisfaction scores, health outcomes, and operational efficiency. Since introducing these changes, they have consistently achieved high patient satisfaction scores, with many of their hospitals ranking in the top 10% nationally. In fact, Shadyside Hospital received a patient satisfaction score of 91.4%, placing it in the 97th percentile among hospitals nationally.

UPMC's focus on patient *safety and quality* care has led to a noteworthy drop in hospital-acquired infections, too. Between 2007 and 2013, UPMC achieved a 22% reduction in central line-associated bloodstream infections (CLABSI) and a 31% decrease in catheter-associated urinary tract infections (CAUTI).

UPMC's patient-centered approach to *medication management* led to improved medication adherence among patients. In a study published in the *Journal of General Internal Medicine*, researchers found that patients who received *personalized* medication counseling had a 17% higher medication adherence rate compared to patients who did not receive the intervention.

By reducing hospital-acquired infections and readmissions and by improving overall patient outcomes, UPMC achieved significant cost savings. In 2019, leaders reported its value-based care initiatives had resulted in $120 million in cost savings over a three-year period. These *quantitative* results demonstrate the tangible benefits of a successful patient-centered approach to healthcare delivery, but it did more. The hospitals also reported intangible gains like increased employee satisfaction, which reduced burnout, and stronger patient-provider relationships. Improved communication explains both the quantitative and qualitative gains.

―――――――――

CHANGE WHEN PATIENTS' RECOMMENDATIONS INDICATE YOU SHOULD

The data clearly indicate that to prioritize patient-centered care, healthcare organizations should make changes—major changes. Regularly assessing and improving care delivery based on patient feedback and outcomes clearly helped UPMC. Once they knew what patients wanted and needed, they provided training on effective communication and shared decision-making and implemented technological solutions that facilitated patient access to health information. By doing so, they *fostered a culture* that values patient perspectives and experiences.

That's what Dr. Peter L. Slavin, who was president of Massachusetts General Hospital (MGH) from 2003 to 2021, did when he introduced the "Ask Allan" program. During his tenure at the hospital, Dr. Slavin received and responded to more than 4,000 emails from patients and their families. Prior to "Ask Allan," MGH's patient advocacy department typically took 28 days to respond to patient complaints. With the introduction of the program, the response time significantly decreased, with Dr. Slavin often responding within 24 hours.

When hospital executives hear complaints and suggestions and respond immediately, they have a better idea about what needs to change. This can lead to reduced healthcare costs when everyone focuses on prevention, early intervention, and care coordination. This reduces unnecessary tests, treatments, and hospitalizations, which lowers overall healthcare costs for both patients and the healthcare system.

Data show that patients who receive high-quality, personalized care are more likely to return to the same hospital for future healthcare needs and recommend it to family and friends. This helps hospitals build a strong reputation and maintain a loyal patient base.

Many healthcare accreditation organizations and regulatory bodies, such as the Joint Commission and the Centers for Medicare & Medicaid Services (CMS), have incorporated patient-centered care standards into their requirements. By prioritizing patient-centered care, hospitals ensure compliance with these regulations and maintain their accreditation status. Hospitals also position themselves as leaders in healthcare reform and adapt to changing reimbursement models, which can only be good news for hospitals that get paid for the work they do.

MAKE DECISIONS THAT REFLECT THE BEST INTERESTS OF THE PATIENT

In Chapter 11, we point out the financial benefits of developing policies like "discharge before noon," which can have substantial cost-savings benefits related to improved patient flow, increased hospital capacity, and enhanced operational efficiency. However, "discharge before noon" policies can conflict with "patient-specific discharge goals." Discharging before noon may undermine the achievement of these patient-specific goals, such as ensuring patients have the necessary support and resources to manage their condition at home.

Making decisions that reflect the best interest of the *individual* patient while considering the best interests of *all* patients requires Solomon-like wisdom. On the one hand, healthcare providers should acknowledge and address patients' anxiety and fears and recognizing the role of family and friends in a patient's care and recovery can significantly improve outcomes.

Prioritizing time over individual needs aims to streamline hospital operations and free up beds for new admissions. For example, in 2022, Huntington Health, an affiliate of Cedar Sinai Hospital, implemented a discharge time of 2 pm and assigned a person to schedule discharges so that everyone didn't leave at once. This resulted in ER diversions to other hospitals from 78% to 3% and improved admissions by 3.2% during that same period.

To mitigate these potential conflicts, hospitals must balance efficiency with patient-centered care. This may involve setting realistic discharge time goals that allow *flexibility* based on individual patient needs, fostering a culture of patient safety, and ensuring adequate staffing and resources to support the discharge planning process. By integrating patient-specific goals with streamlined operations, hospitals can work toward achieving timely discharges while still prioritizing the unique needs of each patient.

CONCLUSION

Prioritizing patient-centered care is not just a trend; it's a fundamental shift in how healthcare *providers* approach healthcare *delivery*. By placing patients squarely at the center of their care, executives can create a more effective, efficient, and compassionate healthcare system. As they continue to face complex healthcare challenges, embracing patient-centered care will be crucial in improving health outcomes and ensuring that our healthcare system truly serves the needs of those it aspires to help.

Section Three

Talent

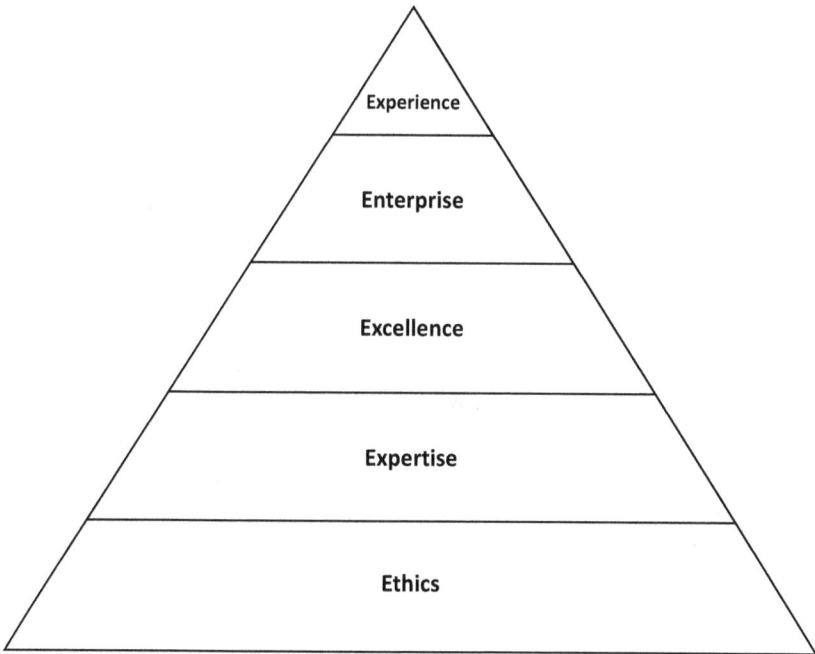

Today's economy does not allow for mediocrity. If your hospital doesn't have the best people delivering your services, your competition will. Peter Drucker pointed out decades ago that the ability to make good decisions regarding people represents the last reliable sources of *competitive advantage*, since very few healthcare organizations excel in this arena. Now, more than ever, the single most important driver of organizational performance is talent—but not just any talent—*stars*. Only those healthcare organizations that comb the planet for the experts, prodigies, and geniuses can hope to lead the industry into the future.

Understanding stars and virtuosity does not involve binary thinking, that is, a person either is or is not a star. When compared to other high school players, by all objective criteria, we might consider an outstanding high school baseball player a great athlete. However, when contrasting him to college, minor league, or major league players, the evaluator might reach a different conclusion.

Similarly, a person could argue that all players in the major leagues have distinguished themselves by they made it that far. But even in the last game of the World Series, players continue to differentiate themselves, when one player responds favorably to pressure, and the other fumbles at a critical time. Only one takes home the coveted MVP title, whatever the sport.

You have probably already spotted the "high potentials" in your organization. These people have shown consistently over time that they can be counted on to deliver results. Perhaps they even represent the best your hospital has ever employed. In other words, when playing in the league they've always been in, they set themselves apart from the average employee. You're glad to have them, and you'd hire them again without hesitation. The question we ask our clients who have an aggressive growth strategy challenges some different thinking: "They got you *here*, but can they get you *there*?" In other words, top performance exists *on a continuum*. They may be the best you've ever had, but do they represent the best your competition has ever had or will have?

Maybe your high potentials are good enough to keep you in the game. And maybe not. Some of your high potentials may well have the capacity to one day claim virtuoso status. They may have raw talent, a commitment to excellence, and the resolve to develop both themselves and the organization. But you need to see the evidence. You need to see *proof* that they can learn quickly and advance rapidly, both in terms of responsibility and skill acquisition. Only then can you be optimistic that you have the right people.

Stars distinguish themselves and exemplify the E^5 *Star Performer Model*: Ethics, Expertise, Excellence, Enterprise, and Experience. They force people to take them seriously. They don't raise the bar—they set it for everyone else. They serve as gold standards of what people should strive to be and attain. If you were to scour the world, you'd be hard-pressed to find people who do their jobs better. You wouldn't hesitate to hire them again, and you'd be crushed if you found out they were leaving.

Because they are thought leaders, others look to these virtuosos for guidance and example. Often, they consider them edgy and contrarian, but they seldom ignore them. Virtuosos chafe at too much supervision or tight controls—fortunately, they need neither. They constantly search for the new horizon and welcome the unforeseen challenges. No synonym for the word "virtuoso" exists. Some might substitute "artist," "expert," or "musician," but these don't suffice. Many can lay claim to these titles and still fail the virtuosity litmus test. Few virtuosos exist. If you're fortunate to have a team of them, recognize them for who they are and use your influence to help them make beautiful organizational music.

Even though some could claim that exceptionalism and virtuosity can exist independently of any moral compass, in healthcare, ethics forms the foundation of both. Ethics underpins all that defines a true virtuoso.

According to medical ethicist expert, Dr. Mary Pat Henman, leaders in healthcare organizations consistently face these dilemmas:

1. Resource Allocation: Ethical questions arise when executives must prioritize certain treatments or services over others, potentially leading to disparities in care.
2. Shortage of Qualified Staff: When allocating resources for medical equipment and ICU beds, the first question needs to be, "Are we paying our nurses enough to keep them in our doors so there's someone to use the equipment and take care of the patients in the beds?"
3. Ethical Marketing and Billing Practices: Leaders must ensure their healthcare organizations engage in ethical marketing practices and transparent billing to avoid exploiting patients and the healthcare system.

4. Patient Privacy and Data Security: Leaders must balance the need for *data sharing* and accessibility with the obligation to safeguard sensitive patient data.

5. Equity and Access: Healthcare leaders face ethical questions related to ensuring that *all* individuals, regardless of their socioeconomic status, race, or other factors, have equitable access to quality healthcare services.

6. End-of-Life Care: Decisions about end-of-life care, including decisions to withhold or withdraw life-sustaining treatment, can be ethically complex. Leaders must ensure that appropriate protocols and ethical frameworks are in place to guide these decisions.

7. Healthcare Rationing: In times of resource scarcity or public health crises, leaders will need to make difficult decisions about healthcare rationing, including who receives care when resources are insufficient. Rationing will include but not be limited to organ transplants, ICU beds, and ventilators.

8. Environmental Responsibility: Ethical considerations related to environmental sustainability and the healthcare industry's environmental footprint are gaining importance. Leaders must make decisions that balance healthcare delivery with environmental responsibility, medical waste, and recycling.

In our more than 80 years of combined consulting, we have found, without question, that sound judgment *ranks as the single most significant differentiator* between those who can make successful ethical decisions and those who cannot. While fortitude addresses a *willingness* to make ethical calls, judgment involves the *ability* to make them. Specifically, the most crucial forecaster of executive success involves *advanced critical thinking skills*— the specific cognitive abilities that equip us to solve problems, make effective decisions, and keep a global perspective. These abilities equip a leader to anticipate future consequences, to get to the core of complicated issues, and to zero in on the essential few while putting aside the trivial many.

Integrity is not a raincoat you put on when the climate indicates you should. It is a condition that guides your life—not just a set of protocols. Stars don't acquire their ethical foundations solely by learning general rules. They also develop them—those deliberative, emotional, and social skills that enable them to put their understanding of integrity into practice in ways that are suitable—through practice. Similarly, stars understand that they can't "teach" ethics to others by requiring their signatures on a statement. Instead, they *exemplify* and model ethics in their personal and professional lives.

Expertise defines what lies at the heart of virtuosity. To better understand the nature of expertise, we offer four critical constructs: intelligence, talent, knowledge, and consistency of performance, and experience.

The most crucial forecaster of success is brainpower, or the specific cognitive abilities that equip us to make decisions and solve problems. Three main components define this leadership intelligence: critical thinking, learning ability, and quantitative abilities. Of these, *critical thinking* is the most important and the least understood.

Dispassionate scrutiny, strategic focus, and analytical reasoning form the foundation of critical thinking. These abilities equip a person to anticipate future consequences, to get to the core of complicated issues, and to zero in on the essential few while putting aside the trivial many. Leaders can often evaluate a person's critical thinking based on their pattern of decision-making.

Most people can learn to follow a protocol or set of procedures. Give them a checklist, and they can execute the plan. They know how to run fast, but sometimes, they don't know which race to get in. Often, these individuals are valuable employees, maybe even top performers. But they aren't stars because they can't *diagnose* unfamiliar problems.

General learning ability, the second most important aspect of leadership intelligence, allows leaders to acquire new information quickly. They size up the new leadership situation, learn about their people, learn about products and processes, and then immediately act on this knowledge. When this happens, the organization responds by moving the new leader's idea to action.

Talent stands firmly at the foundation of excellence, but awareness of the talent must occur, too. Unknown *potential* does little good if we leave it in the realm of the unidentified.

It all starts with *talent*—the natural ability or aptitude to do something well. People who possess talent often initially take it for granted, even asking themselves: "Can't everyone do this?" Eventually, they realize they can deliver consistent, stellar performance every time they attempt the activity, and not everyone else can. Further, once they have identified the strength, they don't abandon it. Instead, their passion spurs them to find ways to use it in ever-evolving new ways.

Passion serves as a kind of magnetic field around the activity or pursuit. Stars feel themselves *pulled* to learn about and participate in things related to their talents, while they simultaneously feel repulsion for some that aren't. Stars literally crave the thing for which they feel passion. Sometimes, this hunger to know about a subject will unveil a talent early in one's life, but sometimes, the talent surfaces later—along with the zeal to develop it.

Stars hone their skills and practice what they're already good at. They develop the discipline to practice, but they realize practice only makes perfect if you practice perfectly, and no amount of practice will help the person who lacks talent.

Some would-be greats have the talent, passion, and knowledge to attain virtuoso status but fall short because they lack *discipline*, which means they lack an ordered approach to developing their talent. But that usually doesn't explain the breakdown. Most people understand what they need to do to change and improve, but they lack the resolve to do it. They don't develop habits that would ensure their continued advancement because that would cause a disruption to their current lives. The rewards of virtuosity lie in the future, but the disruption and sacrifices happen today.

In *Outliers*, Malcolm Gladwell introduced "the 10,000-Hour Rule," which he formulated after studying the work of Anders Ericsson. Ericsson followed the lives of professional musicians and contrasted them to those non-professionals who had started playing an instrument at the same age. The research showed that the professionals steadily increased their practice time every year until, by the age of 20, they reached 10,000 hours. No "natural" musicians floated to the top with less practice.

Is the "10,000 rule" a general imperative for success? Will we find stars of every stripe proving it? Yes. Those whom we consider stars in healthcare have usually worked in their area of expertise for at least five years. If these people worked a 40-hour work week 50 weeks a year, they would have "practiced" approximately 2,000 hours a year, thus supporting the rule.

If you work hard, you will succeed at some level. If you don't, you won't. In our thousands of hours of coaching, we have found that hard work and integrity account for success in many industries all the way up the ladder—until you reach the top rung. At that top rung, the hard work must remain steady, but then talent and expertise start to play a bigger role. Innate talent leads to excellence, but as Gladwell pointed out with his "10,000-Hour Rule," excellence doesn't happen without dogged determination.

Leadership intelligence accounts for success at the upper echelons of any healthcare organization, but no one succeeds without a strong achievement drive. Certainly, the talent to zero in on the best uses of time helps prioritize what needs to be done and the critical nature of some tasks, but without a clear bias for action, movement through the pipeline cannot occur.

The willingness to work hard and a high-energy, go-getter attitude define "enterprising." A competitive spirit, a "can do" attitude, self-discipline, reliability, and focus further augment it. Personality assessments can help identify achievement drive in new hires and internal high potentials, but observation provides the surest way to know if a person has what it takes to get the job done.

Largely because of their passion to apply their talent and expertise, stars eagerly embrace challenges and overcome obstacles. Their motivation clearly starts at their core and doesn't respond well to external things like pep talks, incentive programs, and charisma. Resourceful and determined, stars *invent* rather than respond to the environment around them. They want to do their best work, so they don't readily take "no" as any kind of answer. By experimenting with novel approaches and eagerly embracing innovation, they develop the experience to understand what kinds of efforts will engender the most dramatic growth and change.

When we advise clients on hiring and promotion decisions, a recurring challenge we face involves helping them evaluate experience. Most senior leaders tend to over-value it, especially when the person has "just what we need" in terms of previous employment and industry experience.

Stars offer enough experience to claim expertise and to succeed, but when we encounter true virtuosity, we think of experience differently. We don't want to see a résumé that chronicles 15 years of experience, when ten of those years really amounted to one year ten times. Similarly, a long list of jobs that showed no advancement in skills and leadership doesn't impress us.

But Dr. Tomislav Mihaljevic, CEO and President of Cleveland Clinic, does. In early 2020, as the COVID-19 pandemic began to spread rapidly around the world, Dr. Mihaljevic drew upon his extensive experience as a physician and healthcare administrator to make critical decisions for his organization. With years of experience managing complex healthcare systems and a deep understanding of infectious diseases, Dr. Mihaljevic recognized the potential severity of the COVID-19 threat early on. He swiftly mobilized Cleveland Clinic's resources to prepare for an influx of patients and took decisive action to protect both patients and staff.

He implemented strict infection control protocols and put in place enhanced safety measures, such as mandatory masking, temperature screening, and visitor restrictions. He also expanded telehealth services, redeployed staff to areas of greatest need, and collaborated with community partners and other healthcare organizations.

By April 2020, the Cleveland Clinic went from conducting 5,000 virtual visits per month pre-pandemic to more than 200,000, a 4,000% increase in telehealth utilization. The clinic also ramped up its testing capabilities, processing more than 165,000 COVID-19 tests by September 2020.

In addition to developing protocols to improve patient care, Dr. Mihaljevic also implemented strategies to optimize personal protective equipment (PPE) usage, ensuring an adequate supply for frontline workers. By December 2020, Cleveland Clinic researchers had published more than 500 COVID-19-related research papers, contributing significantly to the global understanding of the virus and its treatment.

Despite the financial challenges posed by the pandemic, Cleveland Clinic ended 2020 with a positive operating margin of 2.6%, demonstrating effective financial management under Dr. Mihaljevic's leadership.

These decisive actions, informed by Dr. Mihaljevic's extensive experience, allowed Cleveland Clinic to respond effectively to the pandemic, save lives, and emerge as a leader in COVID-19 care and research. Could Dr. Mihaljevic have accomplished all this with less experience? We'll never know. The debate doesn't address whether stars need experience. The question remains, "How much is enough?"

Stars bore easily, so they move quickly through the ranks and separate themselves from other high potentials with their sheer hunger for knowledge, opportunity, and challenge. They also demonstrate *self-awareness*, which is a key construct of experience. They accept their talents and weaknesses with equal degrees of equanimity. They know they can't excel at everything, so they isolate those talents that will define their success and concentrate on situations that will allow them to flourish.

Experience plays a major role in defining virtuosity, but it appears at the top of the pyramid for a reason. To identify stars in your chain of command, weigh the other criteria more heavily, and don't exaggerate the role of experience. Realize its major function is to help people recognize a mistake when they make it again, and ideally, to make fewer of the ones they've made before.

We seem to understand, at least intellectually, that we will excel only by leveraging strengths, not by mitigating weaknesses. Of course, we should try to minimize weaknesses, but only to the point that they no longer undermine our strengths. In other words, working on a weakness will help us prevent failures, but it won't ensure virtuosity.

This commitment to leveraging strengths won't happen automatically, however, because our understanding of the concepts tends to be more intellectual than applicable. Too frequently, we focus on pathology and weakness, not health and forte. For instance, psychologist Martin Seligman found more than 40,000 studies on depression but only 40 on joy, happiness, or fulfillment. Fear, depression, and anxiety can mask talent and retard the development of excellence but overcoming them won't create it. To understand and attain virtuosity, we need to spotlight those things that cause it, not the ones that stand in its way. Only then will we be able to develop it in ourselves, in those who count on us, and in our healthcare organizations.

7

Keep Top Talent

From the Super Bowl through March Madness and the World Series, we see examples of exceptional athletes doing what even the other great athletes can't do—at least not that season. We have come to admire and appreciate the dedicated coaching required to put these stars in the game. We have also learned to spot the nuances in performance. The greats of sports deliver exceptional performance *more often than others can*.

We understand all this about sports but fail miserably to apply the concepts to hospitals. Even leaders who played sports in school recognize that the coach didn't play everyone equally. Their coaches didn't attempt to create an egalitarian form of governance in which each person had a say, nor did they hesitate to give feedback about performance—good or bad. Why do hospital executives have such a hard time realizing that their own coaching efforts need to mirror the experience they had in school?

ATTRACT VIRTUOSOS

On August 10, 2024, people from all over the world watched Team USA men's basketball capture its *fifth* consecutive gold medal. Stephen Curry, LeBron James, and Kevin Durant led the Americans to a 98-87 victory against France to win gold at the 2024 Paris Olympics. How did Coach K develop excellent players and make them exceptional?

Dan Bigman, editor, *Chief Executive* wrote "the really extraordinary thing" about Coach K (Mike Krzyzewski) "isn't his results; it's his process—the way he approaches leadership, the way he views and treats his players, fellow coaches, fans, the custodian." Coach K's coaching style may

DOI: 10.4324/9781003596912-10

be extraordinary in the world of Olympic sports, but it's not the only one. As we mentioned before, through stellar coaching, Herb Brooks created "The Miracle on Ice."

Brooks emphasized speed, conditioning, unusual tactics, and discipline but not popularity. Known for his prickly personality and fanatical preparation, Brooks united the previous rival players—often against himself. The team shared a common enemy in the locker room as well as on the ice, but together, they produced a synergistic, miraculous effect.

What did the two coaches have in common? Both coaches strongly emphasized the importance of *playing as a cohesive unit* rather than relying on individual stars. Both demanded high levels of discipline and a strong work ethic from their players. They adapted their strategies to suit the strengths of their players and to counter their opponents. They motivated their teams to perform at their best, often through inspirational speeches and personal connections. The most important commonality? Both coaches started with *excellent* players and made them *exceptional*.

But they had many differences, too. Coach K was generally known for a more composed sideline presence; Brooks was fierier and more intense during games. Coach K built long-term relationships with players, but Brooks kept more emotional distance to motivate players.

Coaching, a powerful skill healthcare executives can use to help their best talent realize their personal aspirations, builds the future of the hospital and ensures more success. Like the great athletic coaches of history, executives who commit to coaching their leadership teams know their people—their strengths and limitations—understand the challenges they face and recognize where they want to go with their careers. Armed with this information, great executives structure opportunities so that high-potential candidates can excel and meet their potential; they provide resources and training; they continually monitor progress; and they provide feedback. They spot talent and make sure their stars don't want to go to another team. Mr. Bigman had it wrong. It's not about *process*. Victory has always been about *results*.

How often have we heard, "Our people are our greatest asset"? The facts tell a different story. Only *some* people should be considered true assets. These people will make the difference between surviving and thriving—between outrunning your competition and tripping at the finish line. Yet most healthcare organizations eagerly pay top dollar for *the talent they want instead of getting top talent for the dollars they pay.* That should change.

First, start with outstanding talent, and make no exceptions, even if you're in pain. The best of the best expects to work with other superior performers.

Second, when you establish an expectation of excellence, excellence becomes self-perpetuating. Each generation of new managers understands what top talent looks like, so hiring, development, and retention improve. Tie talent decisions to clear goals, and you have a success formula.

Third, there's no substitute for raw talent, but taken singly, it doesn't offer much. You must also assess the person's ethics and commitment to developing others. When talent, character, and behavior come together, decision-makers can rest assured they will receive the top talent for the dollars they pay.

"Ordinary" just won't succeed anymore. *Hospital executives will increasingly depend on cutting-edge solutions to never-before-seen problems and clever ideas for those recurring headaches that have always plagued them.* Research indicates that a handful of star performers create the most valuable ideas for their organizations. These top thinkers, who also deliver stellar results, define the talent you'll need moving forward, but they don't usually perform to their maximum capacity alone. They are not free agents; rather, these highly talented, extraordinary thinkers need the structure of an organization and effective leadership to do their best work.

Leaders who choose to lead a team of virtuosos need to understand that these clever—often brilliant—individuals offer more, so they expect more in return. They have high standards for themselves, so it makes sense that they will hold their places of employment to equally high standards. They want to work with other virtuosos in a culture that fosters their growth, formulates a clear strategy for their success, and then creates the day-to-day processes that allow them to succeed. In short, they want virtuoso organizations. It all starts with a commitment to excellence.

HAVE QUALITY EMPLOYEES TO SUPPORT THE STRATEGY

The word "avatar" has evolved through the ages from the description of Hindu gods that descended from heaven to live among us to a more modern-day definition that includes computer representations of our alter egos or contrived characters. In either sense, the definition describes that which can go beyond human constraints—those earthly bonds that limit our talent and excellence. Virtuosos don't represent deities in human form, but they do set a gold standard that suggests *humans have the capacity to excel well beyond the shackles we have placed on ourselves.*

Most communication theorists and researchers consider the appropriate use of humor an aspect of communication competence. Nonetheless, one of the obvious and striking facts about humor is that most people most of the time cannot or will not effectively produce it. Most people usually function as *receivers* rather than as *sources* of humor. We appreciate humor as a positive force in our lives, so why don't more of us rely more heavily on this coping mechanism?

Since personality traits and behavioral repertoires differentiate between high and low-humor-oriented people, we know not everyone has the communication skills, personality traits, or cognitive abilities to create humor. Researchers have found links between a sense of humor and personality traits such as extroversion, lower anxiety levels, internal locus of control, and independence. They have also found a positive relationship between humor and expressiveness, interaction management, and overall impression management. *In short, we like best those who make us laugh.* Think of humor as the glue that makes stars stick around. If you create an environment where the best people can do their best work—and enjoy some humor along the way—you increase the likelihood that you will retain stars.

COMPENSATE TOP TALENT

A few years ago, an organization hired Linda to help them figure out where they were losing money. After reviewing the spreadsheet, Linda asked why the "temporary help" column had doubled in the past two years. The president replied that they had experienced more turnover than usual. Linda asked, "Are they leaving for more pay?" The president said smugly, "According the research, we pay the industry average." Linda noted, "But you hire me to make sure you never hire average people."

Compensate fairly. Don't pay an average wage unless you want average performers. Exceptional performers know their worth and resent those who don't recognize it. If you offer them the same pay that everyone gets, fail to give them merit raises, or otherwise keep too tight a grip on the purse strings, they will leave out of disgust for your poor judgment as much as a desire for higher compensation.

Fairness demands that each person receives an equal opportunity to succeed, not equal treatment at the finish line. If your high potentials show a willingness to work the extra hours, take additional training, and attend night school for advanced education, why shouldn't you reward them differently from those who don't? *Only by grooming the top 20% of your employees will you retain stars and ultimately win the war for talent.* Certainly, compensate them monetarily, but also reward them with the best and cheapest prize of all—your appreciation.

Often hospital executives hesitate to address non-productive behavior and underachievers, but *more* often they ignore the virtuosos. When they do this, *stars vote with their feet by walking out their doors.* A-players want to play on winning teams, and they don't suffer C and D players too long or too much. A-players demand your attention, but giving it to them won't always prove easy.

One of the most challenging issues hospital leaders face, in fact, is coaching their virtuosos. As people near peak performance, tasks become mundane, problems less interesting, and opportunities less fascinating. The adrenaline wanes. They start to experience discontent and wonder what happened to the excitement. When this happens, leaders report seeing less enthusiasm and a subtle loss of edge.

You can't fool virtuosos with titles, even though they appreciate ones that mean something. They want ever-changing, challenging work and real authority to make a difference. They also want to make decisions independently. Therefore, *you will win their favor by delegating both decisions and the authority to carry them out.* They don't want an elaborate "to-do" list. They want to take control.

Virtuosos know their worth and expect to be compensated fairly. Even though star performers don't usually count compensation as their *main* reasons for taking or leaving a job, they do have a sense of fair play and want to be rewarded for who and what they are. They have an accurate sense of their own worth and will resent those who don't share their perceptions.

CREATE OPPORTUNITIES TO ATTRACT AND RETAIN TOP TALENT

Virtuosos thrive most from doing a job exceptionally well. So, provide opportunities for them to specialize and improve. Top performers tend to learn quickly and eagerly, so the benefits will quickly become apparent. When you provide opportunities for them to leverage their strengths, they get excited and feel motivated. Here's what we've seen in our healthcare clients:

- Clever people learn quickly, so they bore easily. About the time they master a skill set, they itch to move on and start to take the recruiters' calls. *Don't assume virtuosos will need to follow the same timeline that others before them required.* Let them set their own pace, but keep the challenges coming.
- They require other A-players on their team. Make your organization a place where the clever choose to work, and your *stars will become your best magnets for other top performers.*
- Celebrate innovation and experimentation, even when that means occasional failure.
- Clever people like to create. Give them that chance.
- Top performers don't respond well to autocratic leadership. Nor do they appreciate laissez-fair leadership. They want direction but in the form of democratic guidance, not an absence of direction.
- Try to micromanage a clever just a little, and you will lose that person.
- A-players want access—to you, your board, investors, and anyone else who is important to the hospital. Let them attend meetings that will prepare them for the *next* job, not the one they have.
- Virtuosos value expressions of appreciation, but unless you offer it sincerely and specifically, they will dismiss it. Most of them don't need praise because they hold themselves to high standards of performance, so they know when they have done a good job. They just like hearing that their boss thinks so, too.
- The best and brightest lead with strategy, not tactics. Often, in fact, they lack strong detail orientation and need others to keep them on track.

DEVELOP A PERFORMANCE APPRAISAL
SYSTEM THAT RETAINS THE BEST PEOPLE

We help clients select and develop A-players. These virtuosos embody the aptitude, behaviors, and attitude of stars. Sometimes, they lack experience, but since they are so clever and learn so quickly, gaining requisite experience seldom stands in their way. We have found, however, that most leaders don't know how to coach them, even if they themselves would be counted as stars.

Model the management behavior you want others to emulate. Give feedback, delegate, and conduct performance reviews. Don't micromanage. Communicate, set timeframes, establish goals, and get out of the way. Talk to them about *what* needs to be done but let them decide *how* they will go about it. Delegate everything that you don't have to do yourself. Let them make all decisions for which they are qualified. Give them entire projects, not just parts of them.

"A" players want to play on the "A" team, so no matter how small the organization, run it like the top-notch hospital it needs to be. Set a clear strategy with specific key performance indicators for each person. Measure results and hold people accountable.

Establish trust as a two-way street. *People who don't trust their leaders lose their motivation first and their desire to work for the un-trusted leader next.* Be consistent in your behavior, mood, and policies. Conduct your personal life with the same integrity that you do business and trust others.

Learning to lead virtuosos will be its own reward. When you can attract and retain the best in the industry, you can't help but realize success. They bring their own challenges, however. When they burn out, which happens frequently, they need your benevolent guidance. They frequently set unrealistic expectations for themselves and then mercilessly punish themselves when they don't achieve them.

Winston Churchill ended each day with this harsh ritual: "I try myself by court martial to see if I have done anything effective during the day." Like other top performers, Churchill pushed himself to extremes to achieve more. Your virtuosos may do the same. *The world offers a limited number of clever people. If you have some, try not to let them self-destruct.* Research tells us that replacing any employee costs the organization approximately four times that person's base salary. The cost of replacing stars, especially specialists, will cost much more.

Whether the competitive spirit resides in the virtuoso or not, one thing remains clear: they don't wait for others to raise the bar; *they set it and raise it for everyone else.* We use words like "thought leader" or "expert" to describe some kinds of stars. But most don't think of themselves as "an" expert but rather "*the*" expert. In tennis parlance, they "force" errors in the competition and don't make "unforced" errors themselves.

Stars often suffer general self-doubt or self-censorship, but it doesn't interfere with their realization that they can perform at a level that others can't. Often, they hold themselves to unrealistic standards—expecting superhuman performance of themselves. But frequently these expectations exist for good reasons: they do what they do well and evaluate themselves on exceptional performance *only in their arena of expertise.* When composer extraordinaire Fredrick Chopin was asked why he composed only for the piano, he answered, "That's what I'm good at. Why should I do anything else?"

CONCLUSION

A governor is a device used to measure and regulate the speed of a machine, such as an engine. Today, BMW, Audi, Volkswagen, and Mercedes-Benz limit their production cars to 155 mph. Stars have no such governors; they don't arbitrarily set limits for themselves, and they don't let others install such devices in their psyches.

Organizational stars are a breed apart, but they share many of the characteristics of the avatars and exemplars we have cited here. When you know what to look for, you'll equip yourself to build a galaxy of shooting stars that your competition can't stop.

8

Ensure Continuity of Leadership

Mergers, acquisitions, downsizing, and growth all require an unprecedented need for information about key healthcare executives and a framework for assessing the competencies required to lead people during extraordinary times. Much of the impetus for the current succession-planning movement surfaced in the aftermath of September 11, 2001, when 172 corporate vice presidents lost their lives in the terrorist destruction of the World Trade Center. Many of the companies affected that day learned a hard lesson about the importance of accurately evaluating and preparing leaders for promotion *before* the organization needs them to take the helm. Many more organizations have learned these hard lessons individually since 9/11.

Even with the revolving doors at the top of many organizations spinning faster than ever, healthcare executives still overlook opportunities to develop talent from the bottom up, and they continue to allow the selection of top leadership to turn into messy melodramas. Instead of leaving the future of the hospital to fate, executives need a systematic, comprehensive course of action that takes the guesswork out of determining the future. They need a *process* that provides objective, indispensable data to help make succession decisions and avoid costly mistakes as the Baby Boomers leave the workplace and the next generation enters.

The previously perceived quiet crisis of succession is now sounding its siren, and smart executives respond by creating *disciplined* approaches to managing their futures. When circumstances usher in change, they should be ready with a carefully tended pool of candidates. Unfortunately, most of these talent pools are not well tended, and too many could use a dose of the organizational equivalent of chlorine.

DOI: 10.4324/9781003596912-11

Decision-makers at smart hospitals know they must do better. They must assess their group of candidates and their bench strength to determine which people are ready for promotion—to identify individuals' strengths and weaknesses *before* making promotion decisions.

A well-designed talent strategy defines the critical moves healthcare organizations need to map out a clear succession plan and develop a time-line that allows individuals to develop skills and gain experience to move forward. Understanding the succession-planning process is the first step. Building confidence among stakeholders that you are indeed promoting the most qualified candidates is the next. As Winston Churchill advised, "Let our advance worrying become advance thinking and planning."

SUPPORT THE SUCCESSION PLAN

Clients frequently ask us when to start succession planning. The best time to plant a tree was 20 years ago; the next best time is now. The same applies to starting a succession plan. If you start five or even ten years before the estimated departure of the CEO or other key executives, it may be too late. Unforeseen circumstances can interfere with your best-laid plans, and the organization will not face the "quiet crisis of succession," but a screaming one. Whatever your current situation, these steps describe how you can start a strategic succession plan:

1. Clarify expectations. What does the current CEO expect from each level of the organization? No initiative has a hope of succeeding if the CEO doesn't support it and requires a commitment to it. Certainly, the human resource department will probably oversee the step-by-step process of implementing the plan, but the CEO must drive the process. Don't forget the board of directors. Particularly when it comes to future CEOs and others in the C-suite, board members will want to be involved and informed.

2. Review the current succession plan for the organization. Audit its architecture to reveal vulnerabilities. Determine if this leadership pipeline supports the mission, vision, and values of the organization. Analyze the one-three- and five-year strategies and evaluate these strategic objectives vis-à-vis the current pool of talent.

3. Based on this information, forecast future talent needs. Examine current versus required performance, existing enhancement initiatives, projected turnover, anticipated retirements, talent growth projection, demographics, and changing business trends.

4. Working together, the members of the executive team establish competencies for each key position. The reason for doing this is that *key positions underscore and dramatize important work processes* that must be carried out. Key positions warrant attention because they represent strategically vital leverage points affecting organizational success. When leaders leave them vacant, the organization cannot confront the competition successfully. Key positions exert critical influence on both strategy and execution and have traditionally been viewed as those at the pinnacle of the chain of command.

5. Identify excellence markers and critical success factors for each position on the leadership team. Ask yourselves "What are the skills, experience, knowledge, and personality characteristics required for exemplary performance?" Competency models can be created for each job or each level in the organization, but there should be some commonality at the upper echelons of the organization. In general, you will want to address *decision-making results orientation, leadership abilities, and people skills.* For as many roles as possible, identify different levels of achievement and the *criteria for moving from one level of achievement to the next.*

   Start with your most important roles and scrutinize your top performers. Build a talent profile that encapsulates the best practices of these achievers. Any leadership pipeline demands a continuous flow of talent, so extend succession planning throughout the various levels of the organization. In other words, establish a *systematic* method for moving from the bottom to the top.

6. Next, as a team, agree on standards for high potential. Some organizations concentrate on the top 5% of their population. The criteria for spotting a star include the following:
   - The ability to advance two job levels in five years
   - A willingness to relocate or acquire requisite experience
   - The potential for at least 10–15 years with the organization

7. Identify the strengths and weaknesses of everyone you consider for key positions. Assess "ready now" people, identify a timeline for "ready now" in the future, and examine each high potential vis-à-vis this list.

8. Ask each member of the leadership team to identify high potentials currently in the organization and one or two possible successors for each key position in the pipeline. For immediate decisions, compare this list of high-potential candidates with the list of "ready now" candidates or look at the timeline for projected readiness to determine when they will be able to take on new responsibilities.

9. Finally, assign members of the leadership team accountability for development plans for each high potential, especially their replacements, and count the development of others as a performance indicator tied to salary or bonus.

HAVE ENOUGH PEOPLE READY TO MOVE UP WHEN OPENINGS OCCUR

Once again, we took a page from the Mayo Clinic's playbook. Mayo Clinic's approach to succession planning explains how the organization maintains its position as a leader in healthcare, despite leadership transitions, because they have people ready to move up when *expected and unexpected situations* require that they do.

Their strategy ensures a pipeline of leaders who understand the organization's unique culture and stand ready to face future challenges in healthcare delivery and management. By taking a long-term view of leadership development, often beginning to groom potential leaders years before they step into senior roles, they maintain their value-based culture *and* develop physician leaders in their clinical expertise.

They give potential leaders opportunities to work in different areas of the organization, broadening their skills and understanding of the entire system. The strong culture of mentorship and the Mayo Clinic Leadership Academy allow the organization to identify the stars early in their careers.

Most other healthcare organizations, however, still need a procedure for identifying replacement needs *before* they occur, or they will not be able to respond to the sudden loss of key talent due to unexpected changes. Long-term planning for the organization depends on its ability to *see its bench strength, to clarify the direction they need to take, and to provide opportunities for star performers to play their role in making that happen.* Not only does this ensure continuity of leadership for the future; it also creates *current* benefits for both the organization and the individual.

Developing talent *now* explains one of the most apparent advantages for starting a succession plan *now.* By identifying a person's assets and liabilities *now,* bosses can work with both high potentials and struggling employees to help them do the best they can, but the emphasis should always focus on helping the stars leverage their strengths, since these people will one day lead the organization.

A well-developed succession plan lets people know that they are being prepared for advancement, which not only builds their confidence that they will advance but also lets them know that they will receive the needed help and guidance to make those advancements happen. This encourages them to stick around. Succession planning exists primarily for the good of the organization, but when it is integrated with career-planning efforts, individual participants benefit too. When honesty, openness, and opportunities for advancement characterize an organization's culture, why wouldn't a star want to stay?

In addition to *retaining* top performers, a well-developed system helps the organization *recruit* top talent. People want to know upfront that they will have opportunities to grow and advance within the organization. When recruiters and internal interviewers articulate what a person can expect by way of development, it increases the likelihood that A players will want to join your team.

Preventing premature or ill-advised promotions presents another compelling reason to institute a succession plan. Knowing if and when people will be ready for assignments ensures both they and the organization will benefit from their advancement. The benefits to the organization become obvious—it will receive the best each person has to offer at the right time for that person to offer it. The benefit to the individual is a little less evident but not less real. People who receive promotions too soon are often doomed to fail, something that no one wants to happen.

IDENTIFY POSSIBLE SUCCESSORS
FOR EACH MAJOR ROLE

In the past, executives used the terms *replacement planning* and *succession planning* synonymously, but the two differ. We have found that convincing decision-makers to have a disaster replacement plan if key individuals die or depart unexpectedly doesn't prove too difficult; persuading them to prepare people for promotions years ahead of their actual promotions presents more challenges. Therefore, replacement planning is a start, but only a start.

Replacement planning harkens back to the 1960s, when managers at General Electric identified four backup candidates for their positions. GE has progressed past this approach, but many organizations have not. Three fundamental problems limit an organization that chooses this path. First, most small hospitals don't have *one*, much less four, possible replacements for key positions. They can't afford to have stars stacked up in the corner like firewood.

Second, attempting to designate a replacement for a job that may change, in an organization that may change poses other problems. Third, focusing on replacement encourages decision-makers to concentrate on *immediate* needs, not long-term requirements. Succession planning balances the short- and long-term needs and promotes the simultaneous analysis of each.

Talent inventory advocates propose another approach for fueling the leadership pipeline. They recommend gathering a group of talented individuals to serve as backup to those departing key positions. A course of action for identifying talent throughout the organization, talent inventory involves the selection of clever employees to replace key managers who will leave the organization because of personal preference, retirement, reassignment, or termination.

While solid in fundamentals, this method presents problems too. Equating *potential* with *performance* can prove risky because not all high-potential individuals end up performing. Only by placing these people in ever-evolving leadership roles can you accurately observe how they perform. Once again, the talent inventory won't work for small hospitals because they usually have trouble paying their current employees.

Effective succession planning requires a balanced evaluation of talent, potential, experience, and performance. This is the definition we use:

> Succession planning is a deliberate, systematic effort to guarantee leadership continuity, a process for ensuring a suitable supply of candidates for current and future key jobs so that the careers of individuals can be managed to optimize both the organization's needs and the individual's aspirations.

Done well, succession planning maintains a balance between implementing business strategy and the achievement of organizational goals while keeping to a minimum the disruptions that often accompany personnel changes. In contrast to an *automatic* promotion system within the chain of command, succession planning prepares people for present and future work responsibilities so that high-potential individuals can prepare for promotion at all levels. A powerful way to maximize human capital both now and in the future, it creates an ongoing, continuous plan to concentrate attention on talent. It establishes a way to meet the organization's needs over a long period, starting with the sometimes-daunting plan to advance someone to the number one position, the Chief Executive Officer.

A variety of reasons lead savvy executives to establish a succession-planning program in their organizations: To support the strategy, identify replacement needs, increase the talent pool, provide increased opportunities for high potentials, and improve retention. But how do you really know if your current processes sufficiently address your succession-planning issues? Ask yourself the following:

- Do managers complain that no one is ready when vacancies open?
- Have you seen expenses for external searches increase?
- Will you compromise your strategy because you don't have the talent to support it?
- Do possible successors for key positions leave because they perceive no room for advancement?

A "yes" answer to any one of these questions implies that your organization has not adequately established or communicated its plans for the future of its people, both for replacing people in key roles and for developing high potential for advancement.

One has only to pick up the *Wall Street Journal* to understand the depth and breadth of the leadership crisis in healthcare and to learn of CEO failure. Clearly, whether forced out or retiring, healthcare CEOs are leaving, and too many organizations have not developed a well-thought-out plan for replacing them with internal candidates.

Why should that matter? First, your organization will have trouble holding on to the talent you have if those in key positions perceive that they have no hope of advancement. Also, the perception that no one is ready to fill vacancies fuels the *insecurities of both employees and other stakeholders*. Keeping talent in your organization depends on you having a *deep pool of skilled candidates* who have been part of a well-defined leadership initiative and stars who have been given every opportunity to realize their full potential.

Second, when organizations lack the culture or discipline to grow their own talent, they have no choice but to consider outsiders; however, organizations usually fare better with *internal* contenders. Research about the National Football League shows why companies gamble when they hire outsiders.

Harvard Business School professor Dr. Groysberg and his team studied trades of star NFL wide receivers and punters to determine what kinds of performance are portable and what kinds are not. Not surprisingly, they determined that the more the new hire depends on teamwork, the longer he will take to acclimate to the new environment. The performance of wide receivers, who are governed by complex interactions among teammates, *declined initially and did not stabilize for a year.* Conversely, punters, who engage in the comparatively individualistic act of kicking a football, showed no significant differences in their performance when they changed teams. Even though hospitals aren't the same as NFL teams, the principles still apply.

When considering *outside* talent, decision-makers do well, therefore, to ask themselves *how transferable the skills will be* and how long people will need to produce in your organization as well as their résumés indicate they did in their last jobs.

Also, external candidates usually create greater risks because no one knows them well. According to Booz Allen reports, during the first two years, CEOs from outside the organization produce higher returns for investors. But as the tenure grows longer, insider CEOs tend to do much better. The numbers point to an indisputable conclusion: In the long run, hospitals fare better when they grow their own talent. In organizations that stretch their abilities and expand the knowledge of their high potential over a period, when replacement becomes necessary, decision-makers can select from internal candidates that they have spent time observing, evaluating, and developing.

A word of caution: When organizations don't have a well-defined succession plan, reliance on internal candidates can backfire. *Known* candidates may sail through the promotion process when board directors and senior executives fail to engage in the rigorous and sometimes arduous task of evaluation. Instead of engaging in due diligence, decision-makers can allow social and emotional ties to certain individuals to guide their choices. Outside candidates should always be an option, but they should not be your *only* option.

DEFINE SPECIFIC SUCCESS FACTORS FOR EACH LEVEL

Authors have filled the shelves with books about leadership, personality, charisma, and emotional intelligence. Management schools offer classes that teach accounting, marketing, and finance but not enough about what it takes to develop followership, arguably a complicated concept and a somewhat abstract one. Yet, to define what your organization requires, you need an *explicit* list of criteria that you will consider when making high-caliber succession-planning decisions at each juncture in the leadership pipeline. As previously mentioned, there are four major general leadership competencies that you will want to evaluate at all levels: decision-making, task orientation, leadership skills, and people skills. Specifically, *numerical problem-solving, critical thinking, and proficient learning define the basics of business acumen.*

Even though all four general leadership skills serve as predictors of future leadership success, the most crucial forecaster of executive success is brainpower, or the *specific cognitive abilities that equip us to make decisions and solve problems.* Three main components define what we call leadership intelligence: critical thinking, learning ability, and quantitative abilities. Of these, *critical thinking* is the most important and the least understood.

Dispassionate scrutiny, strategic focus, and analytical reasoning form the foundation of critical thinking. These abilities equip a person to anticipate future consequences, get to the core of complicated issues, and zero in on the critical few while putting aside the trivial many. Often, the *absence* of critical thinking skills becomes obvious in a leader's ultimate downfall. If the board and CEO often ask, "What did you think would happen?" you might have a case of a senior leader who lacks the analytical reasoning skills to do the job.

General learning ability, the second most important aspect of leadership intelligence, allows leaders to *acquire new information quickly,* which means they don't lose valuable time moving through the pipeline. They size up the situation, learn about their people, learn about services and processes, and then immediately act on this knowledge. When this happens, the organization responds by moving the new leader's idea to action. Reading ability, vocabulary, and fundamental math skills form the foundation of learning ability. Often, but not always, educational success accurately predicts how quickly someone will learn in the organization. Certainly, ongoing learning teaches people about their own learning styles, so they become more proficient at acquiring new information and skills.

Not every turn in the leadership pipeline requires quantitative abilities, but we find them critical in the CEO and CFO and the people who report to them. C-suite executives must understand how the hospital *gets the work, does the work, and gets paid for the work.* Knowing what the numbers mean and using them to make sophisticated business decisions equips an individual to make budget or profit and loss assessments. Superior development of these skills allows a person to evaluate the nuances of mergers, acquisitions, and risk-taking ventures as they analyze strategy.

Leadership intelligence accounts for success at the upper echelons of any organization, but no one succeeds without demonstrating a strong *achievement drive.* Certainly, the ability to zero in on best uses of time helps prioritize what needs to be done and the critical nature of some tasks; however, without a clear *bias for action,* longevity in the organization, much less movement through the pipeline, cannot occur.

Once people clearly define a problem and differentiate between essential objectives and less relevant ones, their willingness to work hard and a high-energy, go-getter approach define task orientation. A competitive spirit, a "can do" attitude, self-discipline, reliability, and focus further augment it. The surest way to know if a person has what it takes to get the job done is *observation*. Once again, performance reviews and feedback from multi-rater surveys or interviews provide the insight to judge a candidate's commitment to realizing goals.

Even though succession planning concentrates on leadership development, realize not everyone in your organization is cut out to be a leader. Some can be strong solo contributors, perhaps throughout their careers. However, the most important leadership competency, integrity, remains non-negotiable at every level. Warning flags usually begin to surface early in a person's career, but if the person performs well, productivity can serve as a cover for the lack of integrity.

Dominance, emotional maturity, the knowledge *of how to build cohesion,* and an understanding of *how to structure work* for and with others shape the foundation of successful leaders. As an individual moves through the leadership pipeline, the list grows, but as soon as a person takes on direct report responsibilities, this list becomes essential.

People skills round out the list of leadership competencies. Once again, the list grows as leadership responsibilities increase, but as soon as people move from solo contributors to managers of others, they need to spin up their *responsiveness and fairness*. A large part of their job will now involve understanding others (not necessarily making sure others understand them), so strong listening skills reign. Empathy and a commitment to building trust will also help them construct a team that focuses on collaborative efforts and strong rapport, and finally, a knack for spotting and developing talent.

MAKE SUCCESSION PLANNING A SYSTEMATIC, TRANSPARENT PROCESS

Because succession planning guarantees leadership continuity, organizations need a *clearly defined way to understand the steps in the leadership pipeline*. Some experts offer five or six "turns" in the pipeline that represent significant passages that outline the challenges involved in making each leadership transition. Your organization, depending on your size and structure, may define the transition from solo contributor to CEO in as few as three or four steps. For this discussion, however, we offer *five* stages of leadership development that can be applicable to both large and small organizations.

Leadership Pipeline

```
                                              ┌──────────
                                              │  CEO
                                     ┌────────┘
                                     │  Functional
                                     │  lead
                            ┌────────┘
                            │  Manager
                            │  of other
                            │  managers
                   ┌────────┘
                   │  Manager
                   │  with direct
          ─────────┘  reports

          Solo
          contributor
```

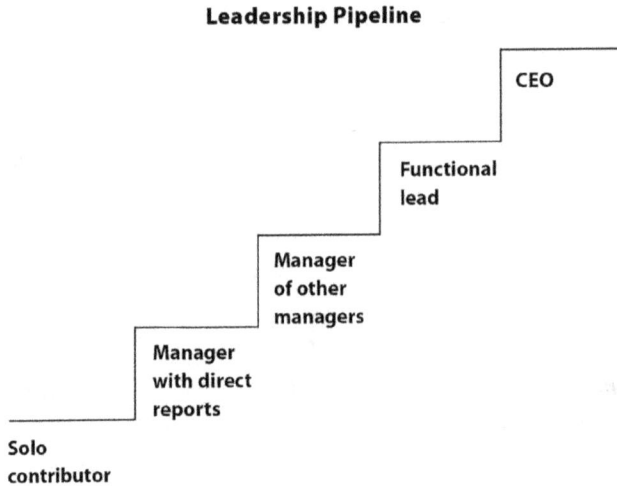

As we mentioned earlier, not everyone can or wants to be a leader. Some find fulfillment in working by themselves without the additional responsibility of direct reports. While many hospitals view the role of solo contributor as a stepping stone on the leadership path, others find ways to utilize the talents of those who want to remain in this role. If you create an "up or out" organization, you will lose good people and incur additional recruiting, onboarding, and training costs.

Perhaps the most difficult passage in the leadership pipeline, the first one, demands a transition from touching the work to managing others who do it. Clients often tell us they miss that feeling of accomplishment that comes from a job well done. They also report that they feel enormous vulnerability. No longer will *their own efforts* define their destinies; now they must rely on others, who may or may not do a good job. Jumping in to fix problems instead of helping others develop their problem-solving skills saves time. Similarly, just doing the job yourself ensures quality and efficiency. Yet only those who overcome these tendencies stand to move further through the pipeline.

Even though the first step in the leadership pipeline, usually the most difficult adjustment early in a person's career, can be tough, the transition to managing other managers offers its own challenges. As directors, vice presidents, or division lead, these individuals will not only be asked to manage those who were once peers, they will now oversee those who do most of the work within the organization.

In large hospital systems and organizations, the C-Suite, general managers, and presidents of divisions define those in the ranks of *multi-business leaders and functional leads.* These people enter the arena of significant autonomy, financial responsibilities, and ownership of the organization's future. They can usually count on receiving much less guidance and mentoring than they did at other stages of their careers, and they often experience, sometimes for the first time, loneliness at the top. Highly visible from both above and below, these leaders frequently serve as a buffer between the CEO and other areas of the organization and must engage in the hard and sometimes frustrating business of allocating resources to competing entities. Those with thin skin need not apply.

The job of CEO is like no other. It requires managing the enterprise in its totality and *responsibility for multiple constituencies*: the board of directors, investors, shareholders, employees, and the community. Room for error becomes nonexistent, yet others hesitate to bring them bad news. Interacting with external groups and projecting a positive image of the organization appear on the radar screen, yet minding the store never ceases to be tantamount.

For this unique position, only those who have successfully navigated the previous steps in the pipeline can hope to do well. But even that offers no guarantee. In addition to the skills and abilities they demonstrated throughout their careers, these executives need to be visionary thinkers who can handle ambiguity. They must know how to grow the organization *organically and acquisitively* and lead geographically dispersed, disparate entities. As agents for and champions of innovation and improvement, they must have the capacity to *set the pace of change and to orchestrate it.*

Turnover among hospital CEOs has trended downward since hitting 20% in 2013; however, according to the American Hospital Association, it still hovers at about 16%, which accounts for tremendous burdens to the affected hospitals, especially those in rural areas. Research indicates that those who leave high-stakes positions cost the organization at least four times their base salary. In a rural hospital where the CEO earns a base salary of $300,000, the loss quickly gets into millions of dollars—dollars that they can't afford—if they don't have internal candidates ready to move up.

CONSISTENTLY EVALUATE LEADERSHIP READINESS

Defining leadership competencies is the voice, evaluation for readiness the echo. The two must walk in tandem, neither alone guaranteeing success, but *together* making it more likely. To evaluate your bench's leadership competencies, begin by collecting applicable data on existing employees. If you assimilate these kinds of data early, you will have time working for you instead of against you when the time comes to hire or promote. In an emergency, if you push to fill a vacated position, you lose this advantage. What kind of data? Gather information about each person's education, work history, performance reviews, aspirations, competency levels, problem-solving abilities, learning potential, strengths, developmental imperatives, and leadership style.

Interviewing and testing provide two ways to pull together information that would not ordinarily be in a person's personnel file. This takes time and will probably involve the organization's hiring an outside consultant who has been trained to administer and interpret psychometrics and cognitive assessments. However, the inclusion of quantifiable, reliable data increases objectivity and fairness and facilitates more accurate comparisons and contrasts.

This part of the plan creates a system for all participants to be evaluated impartially. This can't be left to HR because they don't have the credentials to administer the reliable assessments that have been validated for per-employment and promotion. Using unvalidated instruments like the DISC and Myers-Briggs puts the organization at risk for a lawsuit, and they don't generate data that really improves the process anyway. In other words, *no assessments are better than non-validated ones.*

Performance appraisal rankings should be included in any discussion of succession planning. Cognitive scores and personality data offer invaluable information, but nothing trumps a high-performance track record. Individuals may fit the profile of a leader, but if they either haven't had an ample opportunity to perform at a high level or simply haven't performed, question that person's readiness for promotion.

Including multi-rater feedback results in this process remains a controversial issue, but we advocate its inclusion. Even though occasionally results can be skewed in either positive or negative directions, knowing what others in the organization think of the candidate and providing

feedback to the person about these results, benefits both the decision-makers and the candidate.

Tyson Foods, the Springdale, Arkansas, food giant, provides a good example of how to use data to make succession-planning decisions. Despite its size after its 2001 acquisition of International Beef Products, the organization invested in very little leadership development and had no system to ensure a steady supply of qualified talent. With the addition of another large organization, they had redundant positions at the top.

John Tyson, the grandson of the founder, decided to change that in the summer of 2002 when he realized his ad hoc approach to leadership development didn't work. In 2005, Tyson gave an interview to the *Harvard Business Review*, "Growing Talent as if Your Business Depended on It" that explained what he did. Tyson formed a task force that included succession-planning experts to look at the problem, and Linda was a member of this team.

When you have all the available information, as Linda and the succession-planning team did, do two things. First, separate skills and abilities that can be developed from those that cannot. Then, determine if you need to "grow" or "buy" high potentials at each level of the organization. Coaching skills, delegation skills, communication skills, interpersonal competencies, and performance management skills can all be developed or honed, provided the individual wants to commit to the work of changing behaviors. Learning potential, decision-making capabilities, problem-solving skills, critical thinking, abstract thinking, creativity, integrity, and strategic planning prove more difficult to develop. If adults don't have these, there's very little anyone can do to create them. People can certainly improve in these areas, and with help, they can learn to develop coping behaviors for using what they have to their fullest potential, but improvement will be limited.

Once you have aggregated information on each person, define readiness for promotion. When you have completed the previous steps, readiness for promotion and the speed with which a person can progress should be apparent. A four-tiered scale works well to classify candidates. This is the one we used at Tyson:

A Players are ready now for promotion and can advance two levels in five years.

B Players can be ready to advance in one year.

C Players can handle responsibilities at their present level or one level above.

D Players should be held over or cut.

Analyzing the readiness of internal candidates provides critical information about both existing gaps and ones that will likely surface in the future. If no one can be ready to fill vacancies when they occur, a search for outside replacements may be indicated. Bringing that person on sooner rather than later may cost in the short run, but in the long run, having someone ready for key positions can pay huge dividends.

Train and develop high-potential candidates. Gathering data to make promotion decisions begins the process of developing people to their greatest capacity. This ongoing process can take many forms but should include the development of individual action plans, ongoing internal mentoring, and performance management from the boss. Training, external feedback and coaching, and educational opportunities offer other options. One CEO recently inquired, "What if I spend all this money on development, and people leave?" We asked him, "What if you *don't*, and they stay?" Suddenly spending time, money, and effort on development made more sense.

Track the loss of high potentials. If you ear mark an individual for rapid movement through the pipeline, and that person decides to leave, find out why. If more than one top performer mentions the same problem, you have a clog in the pipeline. Often, their reason for leaving will be bad leadership, either in their immediate boss or in the overall leadership of the organization. When you have a transparent, fair system for moving top performers through the pipeline, people feel in control of their own destinies, and they perceive opportunities to advance. When these stars leave, they often report that they did not receive what they considered just treatment or adequate mentoring.

Objective analysis forms the heart of success for this kind of process. So often, decision-makers focus on what people are like and ignore what they actually *do*. When they consider all available information about the pool of candidates, they can help the organization realize both future and present benefits.

CONCLUSION

Successful succession management lowers employee turnover, improves morale, fuels the leadership pipeline, and places the most qualified candidates in key positions. Clearly, succession planning is critical, and efforts to put it in place should begin immediately, but it won't happen overnight. It will require considerable attention to design, commitment of top managers, the credibility of the planning staff, and resource allocation; but with CEO buy-in and a well-planned approach, you can begin to collect the data that will start the process.

Initially, you can expect some resistance to any kind of change like this because people will worry that they won't "pass" the tests or that they will somehow jeopardize their chances of moving forward if anyone takes the time to notice them. With time, however, people will realize they will benefit from the opportunities to advance. In fact, we often recommend that organizations create the impression that being invited to be a part of this sort of initiative is a rite of passage or a badge of honor.

Whether embraced by all or not, executives can't let popular opinion distract them from the best interests of the organization. After all, "success" literally forms the foundation of "succession." Above all else, realize that you can't delegate succession planning to HR!

9

Foster Collaboration

For centuries, we have understood that a galaxy consists of a massive, gravitationally bound system consisting of individual stars that naturally attract one another. Scientifically, we understand the naturally occurring phenomenon of gravity and the role it plays in keeping celestial stars in orbit with one another, but we haven't used this knowledge to understand how human stars create their own gravity with one another to create a professional galaxy of top performers.

A galaxy starts with individual stars, just as exceptional organizations and sports teams start with the success of key individuals. Pele, David Beckham, Magic Johnson—just to name a few—carried a disproportionate share of the credit and responsibility for their teams' successes. Steve Jobs put Apple on the map and created a company that has both survived his demise and thrived in his absence. Like their celestial counterparts, these supernovae consistently caused a burst of energy that outshone the entire team—their respective galaxies. Unlike their celestial counterparts, these luminaries did not fade from view almost immediately. Instead, they led their teams to success over an extended period.

When you recruit a star, you've taken an important first step in building a galaxy—but only a first step. If you stop there, you won't enjoy much more success than if you'd saved the money and hired ordinary people in the first place. Similarly, if you recruit a collection of stars and fail to help them develop some degree of cohesion, you doom yourself to the track record of leaders who thought assembling some top performers would suffice. Just as a world-class orchestra needs sections of string, brass, woodwind, and percussion instruments and a conductor who can help them

DOI: 10.4324/9781003596912-12

make beautiful music together, healthcare organizations need exceptional, diverse talent in key positions that their maestro can orchestrate to
create something bigger and better. Top performers don't make this easy,
however.

Research offers overwhelming evidence that groups of extremely bright
and talented individuals often appreciably underperform when compared
to groups comprised of average or above-average talent. Too often, leaders think they've done their job by collecting individual stars. Then, they
and everyone else retreat to a safe distance to watch the innovative fire-
works. Frequently, however, instead of engendering "ooh's and ahh's,"
the group—which never formed into a team—causes a hugely expensive
dud. Consider the eight functions of teams when structuring a team and
positioning to create a galaxy of stars, not a collection of gases and egos
(Figure 9.1).

High Performing Team

FIGURE 9.1

BE CANDID WHETHER THE NEWS IS GOOD OR BAD

Candor relies on trust, which has four main constructs: integrity, competence, predictability, and the belief that the boss cares. Leaders must convey trust in these four ways for star performers to trust them. Stars who form teams carry these same expectations into the team setting and apply them to other team members, but things become more complicated with more moving parts. Candor helps.

People realize they're vulnerable to their bosses by dint of the boss / employee relationship. They accept this structure. But allowing themselves to become vulnerable to peers in a team situation introduces another level of complexity. Using the four constructs, then, each member must "trust" each other member to act with integrity. Team members often describe the nuances of integrity when they report that they find a member credible— that they can not only feel confident about the content of comments but also have faith that the member offered them in a spirit of mutual respect.

Trust becomes apparent when members begin to admit mistakes to one another and to offer and accept apologies. They do this only when they feel comfortable enough that neither the boss nor any other team member will use the information in any harmful way. The immediate and long-term payoff is that candor remains high, whether the news is good or bad. Similarly, members will give each other dispassionate, accurate feedback about both ideas (content) and behaviors (process). Don't count on balanced feedback, however. Stars tend *not* to compliment themselves or others nearly enough. They spot flaws and report inconsistencies; they don't usually praise.

When trust builds over a period, members start to believe teammates will behave in *predictable* ways, even when those ways aren't necessarily positive. For example, one member, perhaps the lead finance person, might fixate on the fiscal implications of *every* decision, while the compliance officer can't discuss options that threaten regulatory restrictions. Fair enough. Those members have the fiduciary responsibility to oversee a part of the organization, so their concerns carry over to their team roles. Others can predict that they will raise the red flags in discussion, even when they seem to act as business prevention units.

The willingness to be vulnerable—to link one's own success to another's—starts with the fundamental belief that other members of the team care about each other. Not necessarily that they're protected or nurtured but that they won't be sacrificed on the organizational altar if things go awry. Stars repeat an internal mantra: "If I sink or swim as a result of your efforts, you'd better be a good swimmer yourself and someone who will throw me a lifeline if I need it." When that caliber and quantity of trust pervades the team's interactions, productivity follows.

Building a team of exceptional people involves appreciating how individual members' characteristics and personalities unite to form the unique culture of a virtuoso team. Satisfaction, performance, productivity, effectiveness, and turnover depend, to a large degree, on the socio-emotional make-up of the team. But one thing remains constant. Stars commonly think they lose their ability to shine when in a galaxy—their distinctive quality diminishing as others shine beside them. Consistently teams underperform, despite all the extra resources—problems with coordination, motivation, and fear of losing control chipping away at the benefits of collaboration. Candor helps reduce the chances of underperformance.

Executives who aspire to assemble a team of top performers face daunting obstacles if they don't structure and build the team at the onset. Without structure, a team of stars flounders unproductively, often concluding that the team's efforts are a waste of time. Pessimism pervades. Conversely, when leaders define *expectations, impose constraints, and help members clarify norms, roles, and responsibilities,* the team can spend its time carrying out the task.

Leaders find themselves most motivated to spend time involved with the team when it faces a roadblock, but often that will be too late. A more proactive approach would be to do the building of the team when it's forming or when things are going well.

No two teams, not even two teams of stars, look alike. However, when they understand the universal dynamics that contribute to successful interactions among exceptional people, leaders can adapt and adjust their communication to the situation and make choices that will benefit the team and the organization. It all starts with trust and candor.

ADDRESS DIFFERENCES

Before the discovery of insulin, diabetes led to death. Doctors knew sugar worsened the condition of diabetic patients and that the most effective treatment demanded putting patients on very strict diets with sugar intake, and food in general, kept to a minimum. Doctors and researchers developed the mantra: "The less food, the more life." At best, this treatment caused patients to live a few extra years, but it never saved them. In some cases, harsh diets even caused patients to die of starvation.

Dr. Frederick Banting, a Canadian physician, developed a deep interest in diabetes after reading an article in a medical paper on the pancreas. The work of other scientists had indicated that the lack of a protein hormone secreted in the pancreas, which they named insulin, caused diabetes.

Determined to investigate the possibility of extracting insulin from the pancreas, Banting discussed possibilities with various people, including Professor John Macleod at the University of Toronto, a leading figure in the study of diabetes in Canada. Macleod didn't think much of Banting's theories, but Banting managed to convince him that his idea merited further research. In 1921, Macleod gave Banting a laboratory with a minimum of equipment, ten dogs, and a research assistant named Charles Best.

Hardly the gleaming vision he had imagined, Banting found the lab shrouded in veils of dust and cobwebs, resembling the lab in a *Frankenstein* movie. But greatness would not suffer obstacles. One of the most significant advances in medical science began, therefore, in a substandard lab with bleach, a bucket, sponges, mops, and the sweat labor of two great scientists.

Substandard lab conditions presented only one of many obstacles. After Banting and Best discovered insulin and proved that it could save the lives, they encountered trouble finding ways to purify and extract it. Macleod assigned chemist James Collip to the group to help with the purification. Collip solved the problem by removing harmful impurities from insulin while retaining its life-saving qualities.

Harmony did not reign among these great scientists, however. As the reality of a human trial became more plausible, Banting and Best raced with Collip to develop the next steps. Macleod decided that Collip, as the best biochemist, would supply the purified extract. Since neither Macleod nor Collip was a practicing clinician, Dr. Walter Campbell oversaw the clinical administration of the trial, under the direction of Professor Duncan Graham.

When Banting learned of the plan, he was furious. He assumed *he* would be the one to administer the first clinical test. Macleod argued that when human life hung in the balance, precedence became irrelevant.

Succumbing to pressure, however, Graham reluctantly agreed to use Banting and Best's extract, despite its being less pure than Collip's. Amid this high drama and posturing, doctors admitted Leonard Thompson, a 14-year-old diabetic boy, to Toronto General Hospital on December 2, 1921. The boy received "Macleod's serum," which rendered inconclusive results.

UNDERSTAND WHO OWNS DECISIONS

When Collip heard of the reversal of the plan, he considered it a personal betrayal. Banting told everyone the trial had failed because the quantity had been insufficient, voicing his tale of injustice and tribulation loudly and indiscriminately. Graham encouraged Macleod to dismiss Banting, which Macleod found impossible to do because of Banting's supporters. At one point, Macleod commented to his wife that he should start taking a chair and whip to work to tame the lions on his team. (Since Banting eventually resorted to fisticuffs in his attempts to communicate his displeasure with Collip, Macleod's lion-taming solution might have proved useful!)

During all this tumult, advancement continued on two tracks—research and clinical. On January 23, Campbell began injecting Thompson with Collip's extract. As the boy had been near death, those involved saw his recovery as nothing short of miraculous.

Banting and Best published the first paper on their discovery a month later, in February 1922. Although Macleod had left the laboratory and did not participate in the work, in 1923 the Nobel Prize was awarded jointly to Banting and Macleod "for the discovery of insulin." Once again infuriated, Banting thought Best, not Macleod, should have received a share of the award. Banting finally agreed to accept the prize but gave half his share of the money to Best. Macleod, in turn, gave his share to Collip.

The story of this miraculous discovery, that began with a team of Canadian virtuosos who fought each other both literally and figuratively, has a happy ending; but few involved would have characterized the experience as pleasant, much less happy. People seldom find conflict resolution enjoyable. The rewards came from the keen dedication of the team members to accomplish the daunting goal of controlling the then-killer disease of diabetes. Two things allowed the research to become a reality:

the *exceptional talent of the scientists and the dedicated leadership* of Dr. Macleod. Had either been absent, countless lives would have been wasted until a strong leader could have surfaced to orchestrate the efforts and conflicts of this team of virtuosos. When everyone agrees about who owns specific decisions, the caliber of decisions tends to improve, and the team saves time by avoiding the temptation to seek consensus about everything.

SHARE CREDIT AND ASSUME MERITED BLAME

When members literally don't understand what their teammates expect of them, how can they reach their potential and avoid the pitfalls along the way? Problems surface when members haven't established clear lines of responsibility; they don't communicate; they haven't clarified publicly what each person needs to do—tasks to be completed and decisions to be made; and members haven't discussed openly their expectations about appropriate behavior. Ambiguity reigns and establishes itself as the enemy of accountability, which compromises commitment. This lack of understanding creates barriers among team members that significantly impede efficient and effective teamwork, and the group finds itself circling the drain.

In the world of healthcare, you want *reliability* coupled with *entrepreneurial thinking* and *creativity* that goes beyond minimum competence. You want the value that comes from *standardization without regimentation.* You need a degree of safety and predictability but also the ability to out-maneuver your competition agilely. You want your stars to take calculated risks but not reckless ones. It's a tricky balance, but teams achieve it when they continuously clarify objectives, roles, and decision-making authority.

As the leader, once you have created a culture of accountability and commitment, your role changes. At that point, you should leave the policing of behavior to the team. Peer pressure goes a long way on virtuoso teams. Individuals realize they are playing in the big league and don't want to disappoint the other players. This fear alone causes people to behave in functional ways—or it won't. Either way, the *team* needs to work things out. Usually, tolerance of substandard performance or violation of team norms vanishes on this kind of team. You may be called upon to act as the external arbiter, but when you do meet to discuss issues, reward and punish the team as a whole—not as individuals. And keep the spotlight on the *decisions* the team makes, not just on tasks accomplished or who should be blamed or lauded.

HELP MEMBERS UNDERSTAND WHAT DECISIONS AND TASKS OTHERS EXPECT THEM TO ADDRESS

During game six of the 2011 World Series, Cardinal player Matt Holliday made an error that would have embarrassed a high school player—he dropped an easy fly ball to left field. As he and Rafael Furcal collided, the game looked more like a *Three Stooges* episode than a competition involving world-class athletes. Why? Two words: "It's mine." Holliday didn't say them.

The same thing happens in healthcare organizations every day. So called "teams," which really resemble committees, fail to determine areas of accountability among their players. Metaphorically, they too drop the ball because no one steps up, yells "Mine!" and makes things happen. Instead, members of the group plod along, neglect defining roles, overlook common goals, and don't hold themselves and each other accountable. This sort of behavior, typical though it may be, frustrates nearly everyone, but it demotivates top performers who want to play a bigger game—one where people don't drop balls.

What's an executive to do? During the game in question, then-Cardinal coach Tony La Russa looked down and shook his head. That strategy won't help your team.

History has shown us repeatedly that while conflict can impede a team's progress, overly harmonious communication does not hold the key to success either when it results in groupthink—a communication phenomenon that helps explain why the infamous Bay of Pigs invasion failed.

Toward the end of his term, those in Eisenhower's chain of command conceived of a plan to invade. The purpose of the invasion was to touch off a nationwide uprising against Castro. However, when Kennedy took office, he abolished Eisenhower's Planning and Operation Coordinating Board, thereby eliminating the checks and balances inherent in Eisenhower's

Council. He replaced the board members with people who would tell him what he wanted to hear.

He created a harmonious team but also created a bigger problem. On April 17, 1961, the landing of 1,453 Cuban exiles on the southwestern coast of Cuba turned, within 72 hours, into a complete disaster, resulting in the capture of 1,179 invaders and the death of the remaining 274.

Not only did the offensive fail, but it also aggravated already hostile relations between the United States and Cuba, intensified international Cold War tensions, and inspired the Soviet Union to install missiles with nuclear warheads in Cuba the following year. Why did this happen? Largely because a high degree of cohesion and pressure to conform existed among CIA members, so they hesitated to challenge one another. The group intentionally kept dissenting opinions (when someone had the nerve to express them) from the President.

Kennedy's biggest mistake was voicing his opinion before he had heard from his experts. He needed dispassionate data, not *echoes* of his perceptions. By letting the group know his preference, he doomed the decision. In these kinds of situations—those that require robust examination of all angles—the leader does well to assign a high-powered team member the role of devil's advocate. If Kennedy had assigned this role and then set a second-chance meeting to examine further up-to-the-minute intelligence, he could have saved the lives of hundreds of Cubans, and perhaps steered us in a better direction in our relationship with Cuba, which remains strained more than 60 years after this fiasco.

Banting and Best illustrate the problems teams face when they *don't* address conflict effectively; decision-makers on Kennedy's team show us that *too much harmony creates its own impediment.* Open, honest, responsive communication supplies the missing link, that connection that allows stars to go beyond ordinary solutions and results.

A building full of virtuoso talent who won't communicate with each other won't help you any more than average talent would. If you truly need and want a team, reward them as a group. Hold them accountable to team results, not just individual contributions. Tie their bonuses and compensation to their work as a team. One player can't go to the World Series, and neither can one of your team members carry the others.

Conventional approaches to understanding teams usually address the *work* the team performs—the tasks they accomplish by functioning collectively rather than individually. When you create a galaxy of stars, however, the emphasis shifts. You assemble stars when you need bold *decisions* and stellar *analytical reasoning*—not all hands on deck.

In *Landing in the Executive Chair* Linda used the team aboard Apollo 13 to demonstrate how exceptional people working together can achieve unprecedented success, even during a time of crisis. We recall that On April 11, 1970, James Lovell commanded the third Apollo mission that was intended to land on the moon. Apollo 13 launched successfully, but the crew had to abort the moon landing after an oxygen tank ruptured, severely damaging the spacecraft's electrical system. Despite great hardship caused by limited power, loss of cabin heat, shortage of water, illness, and the critical need to reengineer the carbon dioxide removal system, the crew returned safely to Earth on April 17th. Even though the crew did not accomplish its mission of landing on the moon, the operation was termed a "successful failure" because the astronauts returned safely. It also remains a case study in exceptional teamwork.

In his book, *Management Teams: Why They Succeed or Fail*, researcher Meredith Belbin introduced the term "Apollo Syndrome" for a different reason. After assembling teams of people who had sharp, analytical minds and high mental ability, he discovered that they do not always or even usually achieve the success that Lovell and his crew enjoyed. In fact, Belbin discovered that when these kinds of teams developed a "failure is not an option" mentality, often they committed collusion in their own failure.

Flaws in the way the team operated explained failures. That is, they attempted to function as a team of *average or above-average performers, yet they were stars.* They spent excessive time in abortive or destructive debate, trying to persuade other team members to adopt their own views, demonstrating a flair for spotting weaknesses in *others'* arguments. This led to the equivalent of the "deadly embrace."

In computer terms, "deadly embrace" signifies a problem when two computer programs vie for control—a phenomenon that occurs when each program waits and prevents the other from making progress. A comparable situation occurs in team discussions when people try to influence others to concede the flaws in their arguments, without conceding the flaws in their own. Instead of looking for points of agreement, everyone stays rooted in the orientation and value of spotting inconsistencies.

If executives don't recognize and embrace the differences between virtuoso teams and ordinary teams, these problems become likely:

- Team members tend to make decisions that reflect their own best interests.
- Members spend more time debating than analyzing, so they waste time.
- When you assemble a group of dominant thinkers who have grown accustomed to being right, members abandon the give-and-take required for effective solutions.
- Members spot problems early, oppose and propose, and the group abandons viable solutions too early. Brainstorming ceases.
- When rivalry sets in, members lose focus.

Only a strong leader can shepherd the talents, skills, and egos of star performers to help them realize their greatest accomplishments through collaboration. Athletic coaches do it every day, but other leaders have not been quite so successful.

When exceptional individuals join in the pursuit of a common goal, miraculous things happen, and sometimes an exceptional executive can recast the ordinary into the extraordinary.

TEAR DOWN SILOS

When tackling a major initiative, like a merger or acquisition, executives realize they need to assemble a diverse team of extraordinarily successful individuals—and then force them to work together. A team composed of dissimilar, highly educated specialists often holds the keys to the success of challenging initiatives. Paradoxically, the qualities required for success are the same factors that undermine success, as the aforementioned examples indicate. Complicated projects demand *different* skills, but we tend to trust most those who share the most in common with us. Similarly, complex endeavors require highly skilled participants, but they tend to fight with one another, as we learned from the team that discovered insulin. When success hinges on cohesive efforts, leaders need to uncover ways for specialists to work together, under high pressure, in a "no retake" environment.

What levers can executives pull to improve team performance and collaboration?

1. Encourage candor between you and individual team members.
2. Model and reward collaborative behavior.
3. Hold the *team,* not individuals responsible for outcomes.
4. Foster communication skills.
5. Let the team decide how they will decide.
6. Assign team leaders that are both firm and fair.
7. Stay out of conflicts.
8. Clarify roles and tasks.

Strengthening an organization's capacity for collaboration requires a combination of long-term investments—in building relationships and trust and in developing a culture in which leaders model cooperation. It won't happen automatically, but through careful attention to the eight functions of a virtuoso team and the eight things that build collaboration, leaders can solve complex business problems without inducing the destructive behaviors that can accompany the collaborative efforts of stars.

CONCLUSION

Creating a galaxy begins with a constellation of stars—people whose performance distinguishes them from the ordinary and whose gravitational pull allows your organization to serve as a magnet to other stars in the solar system. It all starts with the individual but quickly becomes more about the stars orbiting one another in a way that builds cohesive, collaborative efforts.

Building a team of exceptional people involves appreciating how individual members' characteristics and personalities unite to form the unique culture of a top-performing team, but research repeatedly tells us that stars tend to be strong solo contributors who would prefer to work alone. Yet no one person can win the World Series, nor can one provider know all the answers. Exceptional people soon learn that only through collaboration can they achieve their greatness. Only then can the organization achieve success that will guarantee that the virtuoso stays and performs well.

Section Four

Build Exceptional Organizations

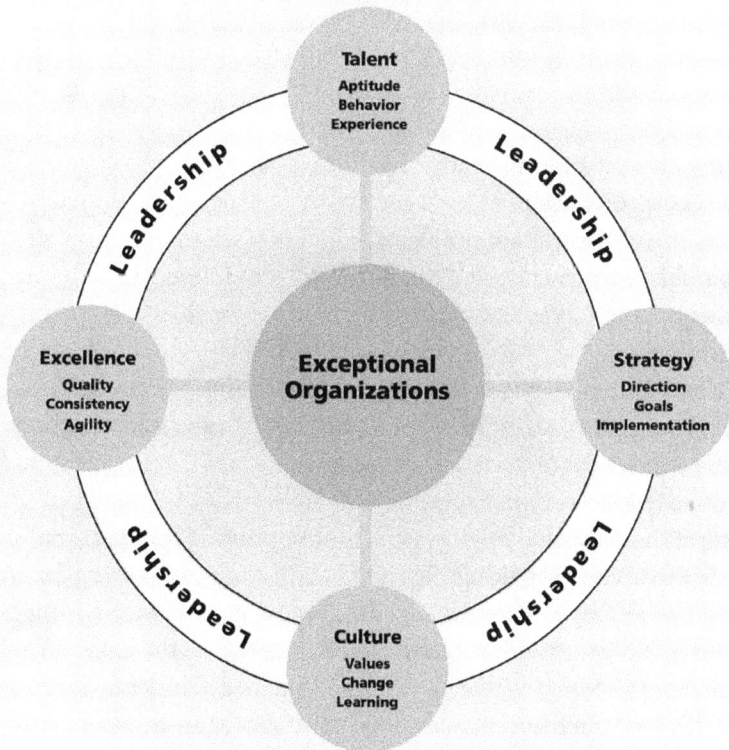

Congratulations on your leadership role in healthcare! Chances are, you might not have received adequate preparation for this position, despite your education in fields like medicine, nursing, or healthcare administration. Perhaps you've even taken a few management courses, but were they sufficient in equipping you with the skills needed to be an effective healthcare leader? Probably not. Like millions of others, you find yourself in a leadership position without being fully ready for the array of responsibilities it entails.

If you possess qualities like intelligence, honesty, and a strong work ethic, this section will provide valuable insights. If you aspire to become an F^2 Leader—one who is both firm and fair—you have the potential to make a significant impact on your life and the lives of your healthcare team members.

Leaders who aspire to be F^2 leaders demonstrate a willingness to explore the essential ways in which healthcare leaders can sustain firm but fair leadership, which enables them to attract and retain top talent in the healthcare industry. One thing is clear: effective healthcare leaders must prioritize both patient care and people skills, which form the core of F^2 Leadership.

What does it take to lead a healthcare Exceptional Organization? It requires a strong desire to lead, the ability to learn quickly, analytical reasoning to solve complex problems, an action orientation, integrity, and people skills. In essence, it demands a balanced focus on both providing excellent patient care and addressing interpersonal issues, embodying F^2 Leadership.

Although intelligence and drive resistant change, leaders can learn and develop *interpersonal skills*. This means healthcare leaders who possess other essential characteristics can acquire the skills most likely to have a profound impact on their success.

One of the most challenging aspects of improving interpersonal skills in healthcare involves striking the right balance between caring for employees and achieving results. Healthcare leaders must have a strong bias for action, which entails taking control and influencing the patient-care team to provide the best possible care. These leaders guide, lead, persuade, and drive teams to achieve outstanding patient outcomes, while improving efficient and effective systems.

These leaders must also genuinely care about the well-being of patients and the healthcare professionals who provide that care. Balancing dominance and responsiveness in healthcare leadership requires ongoing adjustments, even for seasoned leaders. These strategies can help:

- Demand excellent patient care outcomes by actively insisting on teamwork.
- Set high standards and require evidence-based approaches.
- Take the time to understand your healthcare team members individually, including their strengths, weaknesses and motivations; and tailor your interactions accordingly.
- Foster a collaborative mindset where everyone focuses on providing the best possible care.
- Show genuine concern and responsiveness by working collaboratively with your team to address *their* concerns while aligning them with the *organization's* goals.
- Address disagreements and issues promptly, rather than letting them fester until they become crises.

When leaders sustain a commitment to excellent patient care and prioritize the well-being of the healthcare team, they take significant steps toward building trust, a fundamental component of strong healthcare leadership. While personal integrity is essential for establishing a trustworthy healthcare organization, it alone won't be sufficient. It's equally crucial to *demonstrate* behaviors that reflect that integrity. We call those actions F^2 Leadership.

10

Lead

As Baby Boomers retire, Generation Xers look forward to filling the vacant corner offices. The next generation of executives will face unprecedented challenges in the war for talent, ones complicated by a challenging economy, expansion, decreasing availability, and readiness of employees schooled in science, finance, and advanced technology. The pool of average workers may swell, but as job markets tighten, the buyers' market for "A" players won't change—at least not for the better—for organizations wanting to hire them. Average players will be scarce; stars will be rare.

Unless they can enjoy a substantial gain, usually 20% or more, people prefer to stay with a trusted leader; but in a good economy, a disgruntled employee will leave for as little as a 5% increase or no increase at all. "A bad boss," the reason most employees leave accounts for more departure than anything else. When valued employees depart, however, fewer top performers will surface to fill key positions. The competition for top talent will continue to escalate, but only those organizations that have hired magnetic executives that no one wants to leave will be able to compete. To keep top talent inside their doors, executives learn that they must better understand leadership, their changing responsibilities, and the forces that will stack up against them.

FOCUS ON STRATEGY

What accounts for the difference between the leader who rises steadily through the ranks of an organization versus the derailed executive whose career mysteriously jumps the track short of expectations? If people find

DOI: 10.4324/9781003596912-14

the fast track in the first place, they know how to get the job done, have shown themselves to be honorable, and offer enough intellectual acumen to succeed. When a leader offers all these and still fails, suspect flawed decision-making as the culprit.

The Situational Leadership Theories of the 1960s started the discussion of leadership style, offering that effective leadership depends on a particular set of circumstances that should guide leaders to determine the optimum amount of direction and socio-emotional support they must provide. These theorists dispelled the notion that task and relationship define either/or styles of leadership. Instead, leadership style should be viewed as existing on a continuum, moving from very authoritarian leadership at one end to very democratic leadership behavior at the other.

Situational Leadership theorists collectively contend that the successful leader adapts to the unique demands of an ever-changing organization by diagnosing the needs and wants of followers and then reacting accordingly, remembering all the while that the group is becoming more experienced and less dependent on direction. While sound in their foundation, the theories lack pragmatism in their approach, so beleaguered executives, looking for a model to help them, become hopelessly lost. What's a leader to do? Peter Drucker said, "There is surely nothing quite so useless as doing with great efficiency what should not be done at all," which highlights the confusion between effectiveness and efficiency—between doing the right things and doing things right.

Productive executives realize they can't do it all. Hours in the day, energy level, budgets, and support—just to name a few—interfere. Prioritizing *mission-critical* and what's *nice to do*, therefore, separates those who rise to the top and those who fall. Several reasons explain an otherwise effective executive's inability to prioritize: a belief that everything's equally important, an addiction to activity, poor time management, and an unwillingness to set boundaries. Without clear priorities leaders create activity traps for their teams. In these cases, everyone works long hours trying to make virtually everything perfect, but nothing important gets done—largely because everyone is too worn out from addressing *inconsequential* activities to work on the critical ones. Even though a commitment to excellence distinguishes the average executive from the successful one, an inability to make distinctions among tasks and a predisposition to perfectionism create the slippery slope for an executive's derailment.

Perfectionism, an overuse of detail orientation to the point that it causes analysis paralysis, contributes mightily to failure. Successful executives have a keen eye for essential details but don't usually concern themselves with the unimportant ones. Instead, they zero in on what needs to be done and demand accuracy and precision on those things that truly matter— those things that don't squander their time and that of others.

Few things in life need to be perfect, yet many focused and determined executives mistakenly believe the adage, "If it's worth doing, it's worth doing well." Most strategic things don't need to be perfect; some things just need to be done. When you're 80% ready, move. The time you spend gathering the data for the other 20% accuracy may be the critical time it took your competitor to launch the new product, initiative, or service. Think of perfectionism and recklessness on a continuum, neither extreme offering the best course of action. Neither folly nor precision defines great business decisions; bold innovation does.

DRIVE THE STRATEGY

The F^2 Leadership Model explains the *behaviors*—not skills, talents, attitudes, situations, or preferences—executives need to display to drive the strategy. F^2 leaders have a balanced concern for task accomplishment and people issues. These firm but fair leaders, whom others trust, commit themselves to both building relationships while driving the strategy (Figure 10.1).

The model sets tension between opposing forces—firmness and fairness—to provide understanding and direction. In general, the model simplifies the way we think about the dynamic and complex dilemmas that characterize leadership style. It challenges us to ask ourselves how to have both a clear strategy and an appreciation for the people who achieve the results.

The F^2 Model urges executives to use this framework to explore—to gain deeper meaning and arrive at more informed choices about style. This model keeps the executive's focus on those who count—the people in the organization who define success. It helps leaders figure out whether they are losing balance, tending to act like Genghis Khan or Mr. Rogers.

The four-quadrant model is both *prescriptive* and *descriptive*. It allows leaders to understand their own behavior relative to their direct reports,

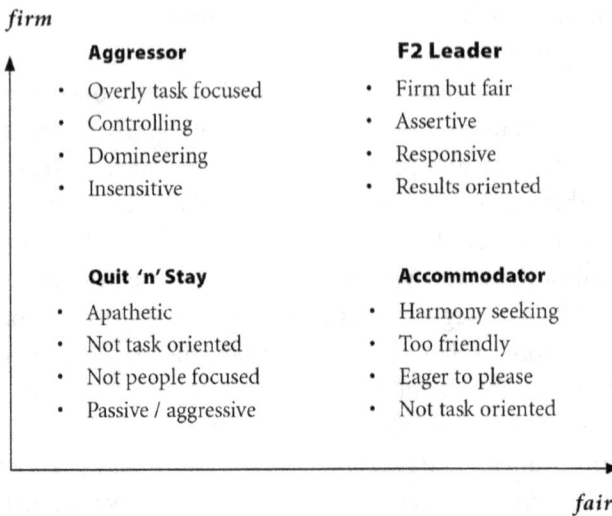

firm

Aggressor	F2 Leader
• Overly task focused	• Firm but fair
• Controlling	• Assertive
• Domineering	• Responsive
• Insensitive	• Results oriented

Quit 'n' Stay	Accommodator
• Apathetic	• Harmony seeking
• Not task oriented	• Too friendly
• Not people focused	• Eager to please
• Passive / aggressive	• Not task oriented

fair

FIGURE 10.1

but by its nature, it implies a preferred way of behaving. In other words, the model explains what leaders *should* do to be effective instead of merely describing what they tend to do or prefer to do. It explores two key dimensions of leadership: relationship behaviors, like fairness, and strategy-driving behaviors, like firmness. When leaders lose the balance between fairness and firmness, they lose their effectiveness and compromise that of their teams. The model helps them analyze what they're doing and then make choices to move toward F^2 behavior. Keep in mind, the model represents an *ideal*, so no person fits into one quadrant all the time. Leaders who want to be more magnetic strive for F^2 behavior, but they occasionally drift into one of the other quadrants.

The upper-left quadrant characterizes *Aggressor* leadership behavior. The person whose behavior fits into this quadrant displays *too much dominance and force* and general insensitivity to others. Often Aggressors justify their behavior because, in the short run, it gets results. Ironically, leaders often find themselves in this quadrant because of their own ability and success on the job, overlooking the fact that the performance of *other people will now define their success*. While they recognize their style as autocratic, they see no reason to change. They fail to notice anything detrimental about their behavior, even when they start to experience high turnover and have trouble retaining star performers.

The *Quit 'n Stay* quadrant represents people who neither commit to strategy nor relationships. Cautious, unassertive, secretive, and submissive, people who display quit 'n stay behavior don't usually make it to the level of executive. They tend to drag their feet on decisions, take forever to accomplish a task, and avoid changes that will cause upheaval in their lives. Occasionally, burnout causes otherwise effective executives to start to display quit 'n stay, but unless they recover quickly, this quadrant represents the surest and fastest way to fail.

The lower-right quadrant describes the *Accommodator*, sociable, overly optimistic, talkative, and eager to please. Notice that in all three quadrants, other than the F^2, the behaviors in question are *too* overboard. Being sociable and optimistic, arguably positive, endearing traits, when used in excess stand in the way of strategy. When they cause a person to gloss over conflicts, ignore troubling facts, give in for the sake of harmony, or spend inappropriate amounts of time socializing, they compromise effective leadership. Executives who can't make tough decisions or who won't give negative feedback fit into the accommodator quadrant. People like working for them, and they often engender affection and loyalty, but when the board tallies results, they fall short.

The upper-right quadrant describes successful, magnetic executives. These leaders tend to be collaborative and democratic in their leadership style. Although highly skilled in strategic thinking, they don't step on people to get results. They consistently show a greater capacity to look ahead, to define purpose and direction, to coordinate the activities of others, and to support the organization's strategy better than leaders in the other quadrants. Direct reports, board members, and other leaders value F^2 leaders because they not only get things done, but they also do so in a manner that motivates the people around them. Their balanced leadership style brings out the best performance in others, and accounts, in large part, for their success. F^2 leaders challenge others to deliver their best; they stay focused and demand excellence. They allow the situation, not their own mood or tendencies, to determine the degree of forcefulness they use.

Therefore, F^2 Leadership involves a desire to lead, the smarts to learn quickly, the analytical reasoning to solve complex problems, the forcefulness to make tough calls, integrity, and people skills. Apart from people skills, most of these resist change and development. However, flawed interpersonal skills often cause leadership derailment, so leaders who possess the other characteristic can learn the one set of skills that will have the greatest impact on their success.

Consider Nan, the head of nursing at a large metropolitan hospital who experienced significant turnover among her nurses. When Linda did interviews with Nan's direct reports, they told her that Nan frequently told them how much she valued them but then didn't keep scheduled appointments, took calls during meetings, and showed up late for meetings, each act sending the loud and clear message that indeed they didn't matter to her. Nan, an Aggressor, created an environment in which her direct reports did not trust her, but as they continued their work together, Linda discovered Nan didn't trust them *either*. The reasons for the high turnover in Nan's department didn't remain a mystery for long.

Nothing about F^2 leadership is easy. Probably the toughest aspect of developing better interpersonal skills involves the tricky balance leaders face between concern for people and a focus on strategic goals. Without a strong bias for action, executives don't succeed. But without a strong concern for the people who deliver the results, leaders won't be effective either.

MODEL ORGANIZATIONAL VALUES

In 1872, Mother Mary Odilia Berger founded a Catholic healthcare system now known as SSM Health. This Catholic healthcare system operates hospitals, physician offices, nursing homes, and other health facilities across Illinois, Missouri, Oklahoma, and Wisconsin. In 1960, Sister Mary Jean Ryan changed the direction of the organization when she joined SSM and earned a master's degree in hospital and health administration from Saint Louis University.

Appointed as the first CEO of SSM Health in 1986, Sr. Mary Jean forged a health system that became a leader in safe, high-quality care. Driven by a fundamental belief that all people deserve access to top-notch care, Sr. Mary Jean not only modeled SSM values: she succeeded in bringing change to the entire health care industry.

Under her leadership, SSM Health grew from a regional health system with 4,500 employees to a multi-state organization with more than 40,000 employees. Sister focused on patient safety and quality improvement, implementing a "no-blame" culture that encouraged employees to report errors and near-misses without fear of punishment. In short, she modeled F^2 leadership and the values she expected of others at SSM.

Throughout her 25-year tenure as SSM Health's CEO, Sr. Mary Jean mentored hundreds of employees and physicians at all levels of the organization. Believing in the unique abilities and potential for greatness that reside within every person, she nurtured an atmosphere that encouraged employees to thrive.

Sr. Mary Jean focused on three areas inherent to Catholic health ministry: Continuous Quality Improvement (CQI), diversity, and preserving the Earth's gifts. Her advocacy for the Earth led to a systemwide ban of plastic-bottled and Styrofoam products that contained chlorofluorocarbons in SSM facilites. In 2004, she banned tobacco on its campuses, becoming the first CEO of a large U.S. health care system to do so.

In 1990, in her pursuit of excellence, Sister became one of the first health care executives to recognize the potential of CQI. Through this early adoption of CQI and dedication to improving community health, SSM received the Malcolm Baldrige National Quality Award in 2002, the first health care organization in the United States to earn the top honor for quality management and achievement.

When accepting the Baldrige Award, Sister spoke of Catholic health care's special concern for the poor: "In a world where people's worth is often measured in monetary terms, we see each of our patients as a unique human person of worth who is in need of healing."

Sr. Mary Jean's commitment to Catholic health ministry not only advanced exceptional care, but also addressed timely issues in ways that help to change the world. In 2002, *Modern Healthcare* magazine named her one of the "100 Most Powerful People in Healthcare."

Sister modeled SSM values, but she did more. She showed others how to avoid the executive derailers. Leadership style, personality traits, and emotional intelligence account for much of an executive's success or lack thereof. But executives can engage in other destructive behaviors that cause them to compromise or damage their own chances for success, too. Although somewhat counterintuitive, we've seen irrefutable evidence that one of the major reasons for executive ruin is the tendency to overuse a strength to the point that it becomes a weakness. To wit: overachievers, at some point, can run amok, focusing too intensely on achievement while demolishing trust and morale. Gregarious leaders build enviable relationships but fall short of hitting targets. Brilliant thinkers analyze data adeptly but then fail to find out if anyone else will support their ideas.

When we do an assessment of a hospital, we strive first to build awareness. When we give feedback about audit results, executives seldom register dismay. More often, they wonder how we could know that much after observing a hospital for only two days.

Frequently people know certain things about themselves but lack understanding of how to use the information to change. Self-aware people tend to be more honest with themselves and others, so they start from a position of knowledge. On the other hand, people who lack self-awareness and self-regulation don't know where to start, and egos get in the way.

Often egos show up early in a career, but from our experience, they usually surface later, sometimes in people who had been fabulously successful for decades. In these cases, they cause people to derail at the critical time before they achieve executive status. Sometimes recklessness explains the wreck.

Recklessness and the headstrong desire for self-fulfillment it brings have caused many executives to strike a Faustian bargain that led them in a diabolical direction. Recklessness explains how and why executives fall prey to stunningly poor lapses in judgment. It has contributed to the ruin of religious leaders, corporate titans like WorldCom's Bernard Ebbers and Enron's Kenneth Lay. Like Icarus, who disregarded his father's advice and soared too high and too close to the sun, these once-admired leaders became reckless and fell. But how do you attempt to soar above competitors without melting the wax on your wings? Smart risk takers define the playing field for everyone else by taking *calculated* risks and anticipating the future, not by idiocy and folly.

Creative thinking challenges paradigms, but it needn't threaten integrity. In a never-ending attempt to bring about improvement, successful executives consistently and constantly challenge traditional approaches. They experiment, theorize, press for new solutions, and pioneer innovation. Yet, effective leaders never lose sight of the value of convention, even while pushing for change. They challenge the status quo, but they don't crush it.

Lack of empathy, probably the most rampant of the derailers, manifests itself in a variety of destructive ways. Often it shows up as a complete inability to listen to, much less consider, an alternative point of view. At other times, those who have difficulty feeling or displaying empathy appear emotionally aloof. They do not allow feelings to intrude on their decision-making and prefer impersonal relationships to close ones. Generally unresponsive to those around them, they display little compassion for other people's problems, especially if the problems threaten the strategy. Executives who cannot or will not express empathy regularly put their relationships at risk, causing those around them to question whether they want to stay.

HOLD PEOPLE ACCOUNTABLE

While modeling organizational values of fairness, leaders should never compromise toughness. Leadership involves a continuous diet of making one difficult decision after the next, and yes, sometimes you must get the job done, but never do it unfairly.

Holding people accountable demands forcefulness, directness, and assertiveness. It does *not* require domination, aggression, bad manners, or temper tantrums. Remember, if you lose control, someone else will have it. We seldom encounter a low degree of toughness in our clients, but it does happen. In that case, the executive knows the best course of action, but because that path will require upsetting people, making unpopular choices, or terminating someone, they gloss over unpleasantness rather than addressing the problem. We've observed that bad news seldom gets better with age, however. Gathering data and considering multiple perspectives are laudable but dragging your feet because you don't want to hold people accountable won't work. These questions help:

- How much longer can this go on before we experience more negative consequences?
- What else would this person have to do before I'd think firing was warranted?
- What adverse effects might occur if I do nothing?
- What opportunities might you miss if I do nothing?

We asked the CEO of a specialty hospital these questions. The Head of Nursing, Bev, dropped the ball time after time. The CEO knew, and we reminded her, that Bev made too many mistakes, and the hospital needed to start the search for a replacement. The CEO had a personal relationship with Bev and hated to turn on a friend. Finally, during a weekend shift, Bev made a decision that put the hospital at risk and threatened a lawsuit that would have closed the doors of the hospital. The CEO called Linda, who was on vacation, to ask her what to do. Linda asked only one of these questions: "What else will Bev have to do before you fire her?" Bev was gone the next day.

Answering these questions when you face tough calls helps you view the situation *dispassionately* and *objectively,* rather than emotionally. When you deal with the facts and put aside irrational feelings, you have taken a huge step in the direction of goodness. It truly is lonely at the top, and often you won't enjoy popularity while there, but if you and your organization want success, it is fair to be tough.

TRANSLATE YOUR STRATEGY INTO RESULTS

It all starts with decisions. The decisions executives, especially CEOs, make during their first few months on the job have far-reaching implications and a decisive impact on whether they will ultimately succeed or fail. The transition promises opportunity and challenge, but it also often brings a period of great vulnerability, especially if board members and other stakeholders expect immediate changes and improved performance.

Executives promoted within the organization face the challenges and frustrations of redefining their relationships with people who were once peers. When the CEO comes from outside the organization, that person must quickly learn about the organization, its services, its employees, its board members, and an unfamiliar culture.

Each person offers a unique perspective, but best practices for becoming a magnetic executive who will attract, retain, and develop stars remain constant. New executives must set the right tone, make effective decisions, and establish credibility—all daunting tasks. Yet few resources exist to help them. They frequently flounder in their attempts to create a competitive strategy, work with the board, and keep talent from going elsewhere, all the while endeavoring to navigate unfamiliar and turbulent waters.

New executives aren't the only ones who need help; leaders who have held the job for several years need direction too. As healthcare organizations expand and grow, the skills that led to an individual's success often won't sustain further development in a more complex, high-stakes environment. They need more. They need a roadmap to success.

In our work with hundreds of executives, especially CEOs and CFOs, we have observed the critical elements of success, both for the new leader and the one who wants to perform at the next level of success. Avoiding the pitfalls represents one path; identifying a clear path for personal and organizational success the other.

Specifically, what does translating the strategy into results require? Executive leadership builds on the traits and behaviors they needed when they walked in on their shiny new first day: good decision-making, results orientation, leadership, and people skills. However, with each rung on the leadership ladder, the manifestation of those traits and behaviors becomes more complicated. Being an officer of the company, especially a member of the C-suite, creates demands that don't exist prominently at other levels. For example, you can expect these:

- People lie to you and cover up mistakes.
- People laugh at your jokes.
- It's lonely at the top.
- The buck stops with you.

Prior to stepping into an executive role, the advice you might have followed may have been, "Show up. Keep up. Shut up." While extremely good advice for a golf caddy, one-third of it is extraordinarily bad for an executive. Now you need to know how to speak up. You need to understand better those forces that will propel you further into the arena of success and those that will jeopardize your journey.

However, no universally accepted definition of leadership, much less executive leadership, exists. Here's what we know after studying leadership for more than 80 collective years. If you were to put thought leaders from psychology, sociology, history, business, and the military in one room and ask them to come up with a definition of leadership they could all support, they'd never, ever agree on a definition. So how do we begin exploration of this?

Lady Luck plays a role in success too. You won't have control of how economic and political leaders throw the dice; forces of nature will work in your favor, or not; another pandemic will overcome your plans, or it won't.

As much as most executives love control, fortune may or may not smile on you. Certainly, the harder you work, the luckier you tend to be, but learning to accept those things you can't control and to concentrate *only* on the things you can control serves as the foundation of executive leadership.

While the qualities traditionally associated with leadership, such as intelligence, toughness, determination, and vision are required for success, they don't offer a complete picture of what leadership requires. In our work with healthcare executives, we have found direct ties among self-awareness, self-regulation, motivation, empathy, social skill—and business results. Without a responsive orientation, people can have the best training, an analytical mind, and an endless supply of great ideas, but they still won't make great leaders.

This should not be confused with popularity, however. Complicated and complex, the recipe for leadership greatness differs. Some assert that leaders can learn emotional intelligence and the requisite behaviors that support it. Others, like the trait theorists, argue that leaders are born, not made. Some cite characteristics like intelligence; others contend that nebulous talents such as charisma separate those who can from those who cannot lead. Whatever your opinion, one thing seems certain. Executives need a new way to understand the elements of leadership they can control. They need to understand how their leadership style may be contributing to or detracting from their effectiveness.

CONCLUSION

Fairness costs little and pays handsomely. Why then don't more executives manage to behave fairly? In a nutshell, fairness and responsiveness take time—the non-renewable commodity that so many executives hold most dear. Jumping in to fix problems, telling people what to do instead of mentoring them, and maintaining your action orientation involve less time than keeping your concern for people as high as your concern for realizing strategic objectives.

But F² Leadership isn't about making popular decisions. As an executive, you will be called upon to weigh the pros and cons and make the decision that serves the organization best. However, the *process* you use to arrive at it can determine whether your employees see you as fair or unfair.

Perhaps the most important step in establishing a fair process involves seeking and considering input from stakeholders. People realize you can't and won't always give them their first choice, but if you never bother to find out what that would have been, you can't possibly respond to their issues, much less create the perception that you are behaving fairly. Listening takes time in the short run, but it pays in the long run. Indeed, fairness costs less than little; it costs nothing.

When asked what it takes to be a superlative executive, most people respond, "vision." Without question, effective leadership requires a strategic focus, but remember, people in mental institutions have visions, too. Seeing into the future is not enough; building followership requires more. Executives who make it to the top of healthcare organizations, and stay there, share some common traits: they have a sense of proportion in their leadership styles and lives; they possess a high degree of self-awareness; they self-regulate; and they maintain a long-term focus. They delay rewards for the bigger payoff. Daunting? Probably. But once committed to excellence, they grow exponentially, and their cash registers become the heartbeat of the organization.

11

Don't Leave Money on the Table

Hospital executives face significant challenges in securing the reimbursement they deserve, leading to financial shortfalls. A report by the Advisory Board indicates the average hospital loses at least $5 million per year due to denied claims, a significant portion of which is attributed to *lack of clinical documentation*. A study by Black Book Market Research found the average hospital loses about $22 million annually to *revenue cycle inefficiencies*, including insufficient documentation, incomplete coding, and inaccurate registration. According to the American Hospital Association (AHA), hospitals spend an average of $118 per *denied claim* to rework and resubmit it. With denial rates ranging from 18% to 25%, this rework cost adds up to millions of dollars annually for large hospitals.

While the exact figures can vary based on the size of the hospital, location, and patient demographics, these figures highlight the *substantial* financial impact of documentation-related issues on hospital revenue. By better managing revenue cycles, coding practices, denials, and physician education about documentation, hospitals see a significant positive impact on their finances. Reducing claim denials, minimizing revenue leakage, and speeding up cash collections boost financial performance, providing the necessary funds for patient care initiatives, facility upgrades, and technological advancements, all while supporting their mission of delivering high-quality healthcare to their communities.

By addressing these challenges and implementing best practices, hospitals can potentially recapture millions of dollars in lost revenue each year, ultimately improving their financial performance and ability to provide high-quality patient care. But how?

DOI: 10.4324/9781003596912-15

SUPPORT CODING

Accurate and complete documentation, the most crucial factor for ensuring hospitals receive full reimbursement for the services they provide, acts as the cash register for a hospital. Without it, getting paid for what you do will never happen. When coding and physician documentation practices improve, everyone wins. Yet, we find that many of our clients don't understand what must happen to keep the cash register in good working condition.

Mistakes in medical coding and inaccurate or incomplete documentation lead to claim denials and underpayment. These kinds of errors include missing or incorrect diagnostic codes, incomplete patient histories, or insufficient justification for treatments and procedures. Trying to get reimbursement from third-party payers further puts the cash register at risk.

While we can't name the specific hospitals we've helped, we can say that we have influenced leaders to enjoy significant financial gains after implementing clinical documentation improvement (CDI) programs and enhancing their coding practices. For instance, in six months, we were able to help a 100-bed hospital avoid leaving $3.5M dollars on the table.

How did we do that? We started by developing ongoing physician coding education, encouraging daily dialogue between coders and CDI/case managers, establishing monthly audits with continual feedback, and reporting. We then helped decision-makers develop and implement CDI programs that improved documentation and coding accuracy, which resulted in revenue increases of 2%–5%.

To understand what that means, consider a hospital with annual revenue of $500 million and a CDI program that improves things by 2%–5% annually. That translates to an additional $10–25 million per year, and the lessons learned continue to put money in the cash register into perpetuity. These improvements typically come from the changes we advocate in this chapter: more accurately capturing patient severity and complexity, proper documentation of complication and comorbidities, a reduction in claim denials, and improved case mix.

Leaders at WakeMed, a large healthcare system based in Raleigh, North Carolina, faced problems with underpayments, compliance issues, and revenue losses. They knew they had to do something to improve their bottom line, so they started looking at some of the things that might be causing underpayment.

They found that errors in coding patient diagnoses and procedures caused lower reimbursement rates. The inaccuracies also increased their risk of non-compliance with regulatory requirements. It quickly became apparent both incomplete documentation, under-coding, and missed codes were the culprits.

Their improvements started with a comprehensive coding audit to identify areas of inaccuracy, non-compliance, and opportunities for improvement. The audit revealed that the hospital needed to partner with *specialized coding consultants* to provide expert training and insights and to invest in extensive education and training programs for physicians and their coding staff. This included training on the latest ICD-10 codes, best practices, and updates to coding guidelines.

They upgraded their coding software and tools to assist coders in selecting the correct codes and ensuring accuracy and integrated computer-assisted coding (CAC) technology to improve coding efficiency and accuracy. They also worked closely with physicians and clinical staff to emphasize what *they* need to do to support complete and thorough documentation.

As a result of these efforts, WakeMed reported an increase in annual revenue of millions of dollars. They weren't the only ones. According to industry reports, hospitals see revenue improvement ranging from *5% to 10%* when everyone commits to improving documentation and coding practices. But they didn't do it alone.

We have learned that hospitals simply can't afford to hire full-time employees to handle all the complexities of improving CDI. When we work with hospital leaders, we usually find that they have a committed coding staff that truly wants to improve things, but they lack the expertise and opportunities. But when leaders hire experts to help with comprehensive audits, education and training, technology upgrades, enhanced documentation practices, and regular monitoring, the hospital experiences better financial health and compliance status. It all starts with specific documentation and a high clean claim rate.

MAKE SURE YOUR CLEAN CLAIM RATE IS AT LEAST 90%

Claims get returned, and that eventually breaks the cash register. In fact, when hospitals fall below the 90% threshold, claims become yoyos, and a situation will quickly turn your "cash as king" orientation into the "joker's wild." Clean claim rates ensure timely maximum revenues and prevent wasted labor costs.

A hospital's *clean* claim record refers to its error-free, complete medical bill that can be processed without additional information or corrections. A clean claim, a standard billing key performance indicator, should confirm the following information:

1. Active insurance coverage on date of service and assurance that insurance will cover services provided.
2. Diagnosis codes that match the codes listed on the claim.
3. Confirmation of medical necessity.
4. Required claim information in the correct field.
5. All patient demographic information and identification numbers match the information in the insurance system.
6. A timely filing window that addresses the payer's specified timeframe.
7. Up-to-date and complete diagnostic and procedure codes.
8. Current diagnosis codes that actively support the procedure codes listed on the claim.
9. Compliance with payer-specific rules and regulations.
10. No duplication of a previously submitted claim.

Clean claims speed up the reimbursement processes, reduce administrative costs, minimize claim denials and rejections, and enhance overall revenue cycle management. Best of all, they improve cash flow and make the cash register ding.

Carolinas Medical Center-NorthEast, a 457-bed hospital in Concord, North Carolina, experienced dramatic results when they implemented a clean claim initiative. They started with extensive staff training on coding documentation and the requisite skills to use the new revenue cycle management software. They centralized the billing function and improved pre-registrations and insurance verification processes. Their clean claim rate jumped from 63% to 98%, days in accounts receivable decreased from 55 to 38, and revenue increased by approximately $8 million annually!

Carolinas Medical demonstrated the best practice of keeping clean claim rates at 90% or higher. How can other hospitals realize the substantial financial impact of clean claims? Start by reducing claim denials by 20%–40% and decreasing accounts receivable days by 10%–20%. This will lead to improving cash flow by 5%–15%. Small, incremental changes can bring significant improvements to any size hospital. Follow these tips to make sure your clean claim record remains above the 90% mark:

1. Keep patient information updated and on file.
2. Verify eligibility and benefits prior to admission.
3. Know insurance filing limits.
4. Code to highest specificity.
5. Run medical necessity check.
6. Stay up-to-date with payor bulletins and changes.
7. Educate and train staff.
8. Review and clean up claims before submitting them.
9. Create a denial management review process and assign responsibilities.
10. Track and report denials.
11. Ensure detailed documentation is on file and available when necessary.

Hospitals leave money on the table if they have *inefficient* claims management processes or fail to follow up on *denied* or *underpaid* claims. This includes not addressing claim rejections promptly, failing to appeal denied claims, and not identifying and correcting patterns of denials including root causes. Investing in robust claims management/data systems and dedicating resources for consistent follow-up accountabilities will quickly and dramatically keep your clean claim record where it should be. Just as importantly, it will allow billing staff to focus on other priorities, like reducing wasted labor and denial rates.

UNDERSTAND YOUR DENIAL RATE

When the CFO and others in finance don't understand the denial rate, how can they possibly communicate to the CEO and Board of Directors what needs to change to improve the financial picture? In 2018, decision-makers at Methodist Le Bonheur Healthcare, a healthcare system in Memphis, Tennessee, asked themselves a similar question when they faced challenges with revenue cycle management, leading to issues with claim denials and underpayments. When they recognized the need for a comprehensive overhaul of their reimbursement processes, they made difficult but financially savvy changes.

They started by implementing a new electronic health record (HER) system that streamlined documentation and coding processes and utilized automated coding software to reduce errors. This, of course, led to the necessity of conducting extensive training programs for *coding, case management,* and *billing* staff to ensure proper documentation practices and compliance with payer requirements. They also focused on educating *clinical* staff about the importance of accurate and thorough documentation to support claims.

Once they had these systems in place, leaders at Le Bonheur, which quite literally means "the good hour" in French, established a dedicated denial management team to analyze denial trends and root causes to implement corrective actions with assigned responsibilities. Through a succession of good hours, the hospital implemented a robust appeals process to address denied claims efficiently, reduce delays, improve cash flow, improve revenue cycle processes, and conduct regular audits to identify and address documentation and billing issues.

Le bonheur more typically means "happiness." As a result of the above efforts, the Le Bonheur system achieved a 50% reduction in claim denial rates within the first year of implementing the new processes and technologies. This led to a substantial increase in revenue, with an additional *$15 million in annual reimbursements* attributed to improved documentation and coding accuracy. The optimized revenue cycle processes steered the organization to faster claim processing and payments, enhancing the hospital's overall financial stability. The adoption of advanced technology and training programs resulted in increased staff productivity and efficiency, further contributing to improved financial performance—and happy hospital stake holders.

By investing in advanced technology, enhancing staff training, and optimizing revenue cycle processes, Methodist Le Bonheur Healthcare successfully improved its reimbursement approach. The dramatic results included a significant reduction in claim denials, increased revenue, and improved financial stability, demonstrating the value of a comprehensive and strategic approach to revenue cycle management and ongoing physician education.

Skyrocketing denial rates compromise the financial health of the organization and lead to patient *dis*satisfaction. Reasons for denials include lack of prior authorization, coding inaccuracies, submission deadline failures, and incorrect patient information at registration that includes medical necessity. Automation at the front end of the revenue cycle helps prevent denials, but insurers still deny between 10% and 20% of *all* claims at the initial stage, indicating *managing* denials needs to march in lockstep precisions with *preventing* them in the first place.

According to the Kaiser Family Foundations' study on healthcare claim denials, 17% of in-network claims were denied in 2021. United Health Care denies about 1/3 of the claims they receive; and Humana, Cigna, and UnitedHealthcare have faced class actions for allegedly deploying advanced technology to deny claims. Insurance companies and other payers can't make money if they pay *every* claim they see, so they naturally look for reasons not to pay. Therefore, hospitals need to develop meticulous systems that don't give the payers reason to deny claims.

MAKE PHYSICIAN LEADERS YOUR STRATEGIC PARTNERS

In our more than 80 years of combined experience in working with healthcare administrators and physicians, we have noticed that often hospital administrators and physicians neither talk to each other enough nor trust each other enough, even though the success of the organization depends on them doing more of both. Doctors simply don't trust administrators because administrators don't consistently include physicians in strategic decisions that affect the doctors directly. Instead of behaving as players on the same team, both groups act more like competitors, and the hospital loses the game to the outside competition.

For example, hospitals measure their census at midnight, but that number doesn't represent all the cost associated with later patient discharge. Hospitals that implement "discharge before noon" (DBN) or "home by noon" policies realize significant savings for the hospital. That means that the average 300-bed hospital saves thousands on each patient and banks approximately *$1 million* annually by increasing the percentage of patients discharged before noon from 11% to 38%.

By discharging patients early in the day, hospitals also reduce the average length of stay. This means beds become available sooner for new admissions, increasing the hospital's capacity to treat more patients without adding more beds. A study by the *Journal of Hospital Medicine* found that implementing a DBN policy reduced the average length of stay by 0.18 days, which resulted in substantial savings.

When patients go home before noon, it reduces the workload on hospital staff during the afternoon and evening shifts, which lowers staffing requirements and reduces labor costs. Improved patient flow frees up beds earlier in the day so that hospitals can optimize their bed utilization, which leads to increased revenue. DBN also helps alleviate bottlenecks in the discharge process, leading to a more efficient patient flow throughout the hospital and better patient satisfaction.

But the hospital isn't the only winner. When hospitals implement a DBN, quality of care increases because patients can be transferred from the emergency department to begin appropriate treatment as new in-patients. Similarly, hospitals with DBNs can more efficiently move patients awaiting discharge to a waiting area. Instead of occupying in-patient beds, these patients shorten their stays, which leads to reduced third-party claims and out-of-pocket expenses.

With all these data from the *Journal of Hospital Medicine, The Hospitalist,* and other sources, why don't physicians more often discharge their patients early in the day? Some just don't know better.

Many doctors assume they have until midnight to coordinate discharges. However, when rooms aren't vacated early in the day, things back up in the ER, and new patients can't be admitted. Patients on gurneys in the waiting rooms of ERs have become a mounting problem, compromising patient care and comfort, not to mention Medicare satisfaction scores. Certainly, things like medication reconciliation, final lab results, unpredicted changes, and coordination of family readiness can cause stalls in the discharge procedure, but hospitals should control more of the administrative and logistical barriers that their current policies enable.

Doctors may find DBN policies inconvenient, but they don't typically lose money because of them. However, DBN decisions represent just *one* area where the input of physicians is so important. For example, hiring an intensivist for the ICU can be costly but the best option for improving patient care, but not everyone embraces this decision.

When a primary care physician turns over the care of a patient to an intensivist, it's a different story. Even though most doctors most of the time want what's best for their patients, if you're going to put your hand in a doctor's pocket, you'd better have data beyond "It's the right thing to do."

Having an intensivist manage the care of critically ill patients is often in their best interest of the patient because intensivists undergo additional training in the latest evidence-based guidelines and best practices in critical care medicine, and they possess specialized knowledge and skills in managing complex, life-threatening conditions. This equips them to make rapid, informed decisions in high-stakes situations 24/7. Consequently, patients experience shorter ICU stays, fewer complications, and reduced mortality rates when a hospital hires an intensivist.

Aside from the financial incentives to keep patients under their care, PCPs may be hesitant to transfer their patients to intensivists for other reasons. PCPs often have long-standing relationships with their patients and are familiar with their medical histories, personal preferences, and family dynamics. They may have a strong sense of responsibility and feel that handing over care to an intensivist could disrupt this continuity.

Including physicians in strategic decisions about hiring intensivists represents just one of the ways physicians should be more involved. Some physicians need more education about the value of intensive care interventions and the benefits to the hospital and the patient before they feel comfortable entrusting their patients to specialists they don't know. Physicians might also worry that transferring patients to intensivists could lead to a reduction of revenue for them and a loss of control over their patients' care and treatment plans.

Simply put, everyone benefits when administrators and board directors involve physicians more consistently in policy decisions that affect both doctors and patients. When decision-makers involve physicians in strategic decision-making, they can ensure that the hospital's priorities and initiatives align with the goal of providing high-quality, patient-centered care. When physicians feel others value *their* opinions and that they have a meaningful role in shaping the organization's direction, they more often commit to the hospital's mission and create a positive work environment. motivated to contribute their best work.

Physicians provide valuable insights into which investments and initiatives are most likely to benefit patients, improve outcomes, and optimize resource utilization. This helps hospitals avoid costly mistakes and ensure that their limited resources are allocated effectively.

By improving physician engagement, hospitals can increase patient satisfaction, attract more patients, and reduce complications and readmissions, all of which can have a positive impact on revenue and profitability. Finally, physicians can help identify opportunities for cost savings and efficiency improvements in clinical processes, which helps hospitals reduce waste and optimize their operations.

Including physicians in strategic decisions is essential for creating a hospital culture that values clinical expertise, prioritizes patient care, and drives continuous improvement. By leveraging physicians' unique perspectives and skills, hospitals make better decisions, engage their workforce, and ultimately achieve better outcomes for patients and the organization. It all starts with knowledge, education, and effective communication among multidisciplinary team members.

UNDERSTAND YOUR CASE MIX

Case mix refers to the variety and complexity of patients. It's a way of describing and classifying the types of patients and the range of needed care that considers patients' demographics, severity of the illness, required treatments, and length of stay. The case mix index (CMI) measures the relative *costliness* and *resource intensity* of the hospital's patient population, influenced by the *complexity* and *severity* of cases. It also indicates whether a hospital has treated a great number of complex, resource-intensive patients for whom the hospitals can be reimbursed at a higher rate than hospitals that do fewer complicated cases. Different types of patients and treatments have varying costs and reimbursement rates; therefore, understanding the case mix helps hospitals *predict revenues, manage expenses*, and *negotiate with payers*.

Knowing the *typical* patient profile allows hospitals to make strategic decisions about allocation of staff and equipment more efficiently. The complexity and types of cases influence the skills and specialties required in the hospital's workforce. Certain case mixes present higher risks, requiring specific risk mitigation strategies that affect future investments in expansion of services and facilities, but too often executives and board members don't understand what this really means, and those who *do* understand case mix don't have the experience or platform for educating others.

Case mix also influences the hospital's ability to navigate *complex regulations* because payer requirements can lead to *non-compliance issues* affecting reimbursement. Hospitals lose out on reimbursements if they do not properly verify a patient's insurance eligibility and benefits *before* providing services. This can result in denied claims or the hospital being forced to absorb the cost of care if the patient is found to be uninsured or underinsured. Implementing processes to verify insurance coverage and benefits upfront, therefore, can help hospitals avoid these losses.

When executives at Johns Hopkins Hospital sought to improve their financial performance by enhancing case mix, they focused on attracting and managing more *complex* and *resource-intensive cases;* and they expanded their specialized medical services, including advanced neurosurgery, complex cardiac care, and cutting-edge oncology treatments. These services, coupled with an integrated multidisciplinary team approach to manage complex cases, led to higher reimbursement rates due to their complexity and high-quality clinical outcomes, which positioned the hospital as a top choice for patients with complex medical needs.

The higher CMI led to increased revenue per patient, which improved the financial performance that allowed for further investment in research, technology, and patient care services. The hospital also reported significant growth in its operating margin, which enabled the institution to reinvest in its facilities and programs, thereby enhancing its overall service offerings.

Johns Hopkins demonstrates how academic medical centers can successfully leverage case mix management to achieve financial stability and growth while maintaining their commitment to high-quality patient care, but much smaller hospitals can do the same. Suppose a hospital increases its CMI by 0.1. Given that a 0.1 increase in CMI can lead to an additional $500 to $1,000 per discharge, a hospital with 10,000 discharges annually could see an additional $5 million to $10 million in revenue. The average 300-bed hospital, with a 75% occupancy rate and an average length of stay of 4.5 days, has approximately 18,250 discharges annually, demonstrating that increasing the CMI has a remarkable effect, regardless of the size of the hospital.

A hospital's CMI is only as good as its clinical documentation. Two hospitals with the *exact* caseloads can have very different CMIs and reimbursement rates if one hospital documents better than the other. Because each individual case affects the hospital CMI, any missed chance to increase a case's severity level is a missed opportunity for revenue not only for *those* procedures but also for the entire hospitals

CONCLUSION

A strong financial position helps hospitals navigate regulatory changes, shifts in payment models, and economic uncertainties. Hospitals with robust reimbursement policies and processes are better prepared to adapt to these challenges, maintain financial stability, and continue serving their patients and communities effectively. As healthcare costs rise, and insurers put pressure on reimbursement rates, hospitals must become more proactive in optimizing their revenue cycle processes to secure every dollar they're owed for the services they provide.

Keeping hospitals financially healthy and stable depends on complete documentation for accurate reimbursement, especially in today's tough healthcare environment; but the average hospital loses a significant amount of money annually due to inaccurate or insufficient documentation. We have learned that by prioritizing improvements in reimbursement and adopting best practices in revenue cycle management, hospitals can ensure their long-term financial health and sustainability, ultimately benefiting the patients and communities they serve.

12

Expand Capability through Strategic Decisions

When things don't go well in a healthcare organization, two interrelated factors take most of the blame: leadership and culture. Everyone quickly jumps on the fault-finding bandwagon to point fingers at leaders for neglecting to create conditions that lead to improvement and for culture failing to be the fertile soil in which improvements can take root.

During his 1840 United States presidential election, William Harrison literally used a bandwagon to rally supporters. This happened during a time when people closely associated the term "bandwagon" with its literal meaning: a wagon that carried a band for parades or rallies. Noticing the popularity of this method, other politicians began to use bandwagons in their own campaigns by inviting people to "jump on the bandwagon." Today, we use the phrase to describe people who embrace a popular trend—like blaming leadership and culture—largely because "everyone else is doing it." The problem is metaphorical and literal bandwagons have no brakes.

When a healthcare organization aspires to grow, instead of focusing attention on the *systems* in which people work, decision-makers focus on fixing the *people.* Of course, people make decisions about the systems, but the systems themselves need fixing far more than the people do. Frontline clinicians have shouldered the weight of poorly designed and unoptimized systems for too long. Before executives begin to discuss how and when to expand and how to do it, they need to shift the focus to *designing systems that facilitate delivery of the highest-quality care in their existing circumstances.*

 DOI: 10.4324/9781003596912-16

KNOW WHERE YOU MAKE MONEY, WHERE YOU DON'T, AND WHERE YOU WILL

In our work, we have learned the simplest way for healthcare organizations to grow is to understand fully where the money comes from—and where it goes—to create financial systems for avoiding leaving money on the table. That sounds easier than it is. Too often, leaders settle for what they consider "enough" data to move forward with the strategy to expand. Vanderbilt University Medical Center in Nashville, Tennessee, knew better.

In 2019, VUMC implemented a new financial management system called "Axiom Enterprise Decision Support" to gain a more detailed and accurate understanding of its costs and profitability across various service lines and patient populations. Through this enhanced financial analysis, VUMC identified several areas for improvement.

Top-line growth must start with bottom-line information. Therefore, decision-makers at VUMC started by reducing *surgical supply costs*, but first they had to understand those costs. The data revealed that VUMC spent more than the industry average on surgical supply costs. In response, the organization implemented a new *supply chain management system* and worked with surgeons to standardize surgical supplies, resulting in significant cost savings. Also, the financial analysis further showed that *operating room utilization rates* varied widely across different surgical specialties, so VUMC implemented a new *scheduling system* to reallocate operating room time to improve efficiency and reduce costs. Just as the human body has systems like the respiratory system, financial systems have systems within systems.

Decision-makers at VUMC then identified opportunities to improve performance under *value-based payment models*, such as Medicare's Comprehensive Care for Joint Replacement Program. These data allowed hospital leaders to identify areas for improving the cost and quality of joint replacement surgeries, such as reducing post-acute care costs and improving care coordination. Finally, VUMC recognized the growing importance of *outpatient* and *telehealth* services in driving revenue and meeting patient needs, particularly in response to the COVID-19 pandemic.

We predict that most, if not all, changes in the future will be tied to improvements in artificial intelligence. Artificial Intelligence and

Machine Learning (AI and ML) will revolutionize diagnostics that use machine-learning algorithms that predict disease outbreaks, improve drug discovery and development, personalize treatment plans, and streamline administrative processes. AI-assisted drug development will allow pharmaceutical companies to use *predictive models* to design and test potential drugs in a matter of days or weeks rather than the years it now takes.

Telemedicine and *Remote Patient Monitoring* during the COVID-19 pandemic accelerated the adoption of telemedicine. This trend will continue with more sophisticated remote monitoring tools, allowing for better management of chronic conditions and improved access to healthcare in underserved areas.

Advanced diagnostic capabilities will expand. Point-of-care devices and at-home testing kits will provide quick and accurate results for a wide range of conditions, enabling early detection and timely treatment.

The development of *lab-grown organs* for transplants will address the organ shortage crisis, eliminating waiting lists, reducing rejection risks, and improving transplant outcomes. In some cases, providers will enable personalized organ development using the patient's own cells.

Precision Medicine and *Genomics Advancements* in genomic sequencing and analysis will enable more personalized treatment plans based on an individual's genetic makeup. This will lead to more effective treatments with fewer side effects. Comprehensive genome sequencing will be a standard part of medical evaluations, providing insights into an individual's predisposition to diseases and guiding personalized treatment plans. Clustered Regularly Interspaced Short Palindromic Repeats (*CRISPR*), a revolutionary gene-editing technology that holds immense potential for treating genetic disorders, developing new therapies, and potentially eradicating diseases. As they become more refined and widely accepted, they will transform the approach to many previously untreatable conditions.

To position their organizations for growth, healthcare executives recognize they must leverage *accurate* advanced financial analytics. Only then can they make data-driven decisions that improve financial performance while also enhancing the quality and value of care delivered to patients. With these systems in place, healthcare leaders can better understand their competitive advantage.

KNOW AND ARTICULATE YOUR COMPETITIVE ADVANTAGE

Any plans to expand need to start with a shared objective about what the healthcare organization wants to accomplish and systems for allocating scarce resources: money, time, and talent. We call this your *Competitive Advantage.*

The Competitive Advantage doesn't merely aggregate a collection of objectives. Rather, it captures the thinking required to build a sustainable strategic lead that forces trade-offs among competing resources, tests the soundness of initiatives, and sets clear boundaries within which decision-makers must operate.

The intersection of passion, excellence, and profitability—your strategic principle—forms the foundation for your Competitive Advantage. Only here can your organization thrive as you work diligently to produce a product or service that your competition can't match.

When companies face change or turmoil, the Competitive Advantage acts as a beacon that keeps the ships from running aground. It helps maintain consistency but gives managers the freedom to make decisions that are right for their part of the organization. Even when the leadership changes, or the economic landscape shifts, the Competitive Advantage remains the same. It helps decision-makers know when to develop new practices, products, and markets. When they face a choice, decision-makers will be able to test their options by simply applying the three-part litmus tests:

- Are we enthusiastic about this work?
- Can we do it better than our competitors?
- Will it make us money or define our unique contribution?

When designed and executed well, a Competitive Advantage gives people clear direction while inspiring them to be flexible and take risks. It offers a disciplined way to think about decisions, strategy, and execution and challenges people to play an ever-evolving better game.

Another way to think about the intersection of your distinction, excellence, and financial stability is to consider the world with your organization versus without it. The difference defines your unique added value—what would be lost to the world if your organization disappeared. To discover this unique added value, ask yourself the pivotal questions.

If we stopped doing what we are doing, to whom would it matter? The overarching strategic force of any organization occurs at the intersection of the organization's distinction, passion, and profitability. This strategic force explains why customers or patients choose your products or services, why you make money from what you do, and why people want to work for your organization. It serves as a talent magnet, unifying concept, and the strategic framework that guides decisions.

Who would miss us most? The people to whom you matter most define the essence of your business. These are your best customers, those who rely on you to improve their condition through your products or services. These same people deserve most of your attention, marketing efforts, and best terms.

How long would it take another organization to step into the void? If anyone can do what you're doing at the rate you do it with the strong relationships you've built, you don't have much of a competitive advantage. But if you think about what it would take for a competitor to do what you do, get your hands around that uniqueness.

Once you understand the nature of your Competitive Advantage, you'll want to analyze whether you're using it to define your strategy and to develop the tactics that will support the strategy. Based on a proven track record, this type of organization has identified those decisions that have led to success in the past and that promise success in the future. By responding to patient needs, developing talent, implementing effective operations, and defining sound financial objectives, executives know what they must do to beat the competition, and they have identified ways to implement this strategy. When a commitment to excellent performance exists, passion and profitability usually follow.

TIE FINANCIAL REWARDS TO PERFORMANCE THAT SUPPORTS THE STRATEGY

While the principles of Competitive Advantage remain constant in every kind of industry and every kind of company, healthcare executives face some unique challenges when they try to implement it. For example, any growth initiative of a hospital must include an analysis of how its Competitive Advantage and Revenue Cycle Management (RCM) affect each other—and how each affects individual and collective performance.

RCM, a complex process that encompasses the financial aspects of patient care from start to finish, must align with their hospital's mission, vision, and values. This crucial alignment maintains financial stability while upholding the organization's core principles. Once again, any change or aspiration to grow organically or acquisitively must start with a patient-centric approach.

By involving clinical teams in RCM improvement, a patient-centric orientation ensures processes and systems prioritize patient experience and satisfaction by avoiding metrics that inadvertently incentivize rushed or unnecessary care. That addresses the *people* side of RCM, but improvements in the *financial* side of the house remain important, too. Consider these eight ways to improve RCM while keeping the patient top of mind:

1. Offer financial counseling and support to patients.
2. Implement transparent billing practices.
3. Align reimbursement models with quality outcomes rather than just volume.
4. Invest in technologies that improve RCM while enhancing patient care.
5. Balance short-term financial goals with long-term mission fulfillment.
6. Maintain strict compliance with regulations and industry standards.
7. Avoid aggressive collection tactics that may conflict with the hospital's values.
8. Implement fair pricing strategies.

A robust system considers the impact of RCM policies on community health outcomes and develops financial assistance programs for underserved populations, which balances profitability with providing necessary care to all patients. All this serves to streamline systems to reduce the administrative burden on clinical staff. The goal of RCM must always be to optimize revenue by ensuring efficient billing processes, minimizing claim denials, and reducing the time between providing services and receiving payment. As with most improvements, executives do well to embrace new technologies and systems, but many resist.

Our research indicates that more than 80% of revenue cycle management and financial executives say they're optimistic about AI-enabled revenue cycle management in hospitals. Applications for artificial intelligence show promise, but about one-third of decision-makers remain concerned or skeptical about using artificial intelligence in RCM. These executives see AI as somewhat untested and experimental and worry about accuracy, reliability, and lack of understanding. Twenty percent of executives remain convinced human performance—at least at this point—is superior to that of AI.

Rather than thinking of this as an either/or scenario, we challenge executives to think about human expertise as a critical underpinning to creating AI models that perform and continue to evolve. To help in making effective models, AI needs input from those with feet on the ground who manage and analyze the data, perform the operations, and direct workflow. In other words, combine technology and expertise for the best results. Errors upfront in the registration process create denials on the back end, but AI can help. The creation of these evolving models helps in establishing and modernizing the organization's Competitive Advantage, but those who drive these initiatives want to be compensated fairly, too.

Like many family businesses, in 2017, the California-based Molina Healthcare hit a wall under second-generation leadership. Founded 40 years prior, Molina had been grappling with poor financial performance and lackluster growth. Questionable acquisitions and a purported "friends-and-family" legacy approach to succession-planning decisions hindered progress on a critical imperative: adapting to the newly enacted Affordable Care Act.

To outsiders, the shake-up that led to the ousting of Mario and John Molina from the organization their father founded seemed to unfold in a manner of days, but it had been years in the making. The board felt the need to act when the primary issue became the underperformance of the organization on a continuing basis.

The organization had been growing revenue significantly, but profits lagged, the earnings profile of Molina trailed competitors, and they missed their projected numbers. These business-side-of-the-house issues led the board to conclude that a disruption to the status quo had to happen, and the board reached a consensus to terminate the founding family members who had been serving as CEO and CFO, appoint an interim CEO, and name a non-executive board chair. Rewarding underperformance came to a screeching halt.

After seven years, Molina realized a tenfold increase in enterprise value from approximately $2 billion in 2017 to more than $20 billion by 2023. Because they delivered substantial value to shareholders, the new leadership team reshaped Molina Healthcare's market presence and positioned it for expansion. They rebuilt the entire team, implemented performance standards, changed the culture, and infused the organization with excitement.

The first step to tying financial rewards to performance begins with financial discipline. Know your business, understand your numbers, and create requisite systems to support them. In other words, have expectations about performance and then reward those who exceed them.

UNDERSTAND INDUSTRY TRENDS

Trends, not bandwagons, show the direction an industry will develop or change. Therefore, executives must excel at reading the *current* external landscape of the organization and predicting a *future* state. *Not* anticipating trends won't work, but neither will attempting to forecast ten or even five years out. Guesswork and probabilities define a future state, but you must also put a stake in the ground *today* so they can better plan *tomorrow*. That's the tricky part. 2023 brought renewed focus on areas like virtual care, wearable monitors, and robotic surgery; but traditionally growth has depended on a more general approach to *delivery models*.

For instance, value-based care, a healthcare delivery model that focuses on improving patient outcomes and quality of care, prioritizes the *quality* of care provided rather than the number of services or procedures performed. This approach differs from the traditional *fee-for-service* model, which rewards healthcare providers based on the *volume of services* they provide, regardless of the outcomes. SSM and others, on the other hand, have implemented successful value-based care systems that have kept eyes squarely on the patient.

SSM Health implemented *patient-centered care models*, such as medical homes, which focus on coordinated, comprehensive care tailored to individual patient needs. This approach emphasizes the importance of patient engagement, shared decision-making, and personalized care plans tailored to individual needs and preferences. Through improved care coordination, collaboration, and integration, SSM ensures smooth transitions of care and reduces duplication of services.

Kaiser Permanente, another leader in value-based care, puts a strong emphasis on *preventive* care, care coordination, and the use of health information technology to support population health management. Preventive care and wellness initiatives emphasize precautionary measures, early intervention, and managing chronic conditions to avoid costly complications and hospitalizations. Other organizations have invested in programs for patients with diabetes, heart disease, and other chronic conditions.

Other industry trends include *data-driven decision-making*, which involves healthcare providers using data analytics and evidence-based guidelines to make informed decisions about patient care and resource allocation. These data logically lead to an investigation of *payment models* that involve alternative payment models, such as bundled payments, accountable care organizations (ACOs), and pay-for-performance incentives, which align reimbursement with patient outcomes and cost-efficiency.

In addition to ACOs, Advocate Aurora Health, a health system serving Illinois and Wisconsin, implemented population health management programs and patient engagement strategies. Geisinger Health System, located in Pennsylvania, pioneered innovative programs such as *ProvenCare*, which offers bundled payments for specific procedures, and the *Geisinger Health Plan*, which aligns incentives with quality and cost-efficiency.

Many healthcare organizations, including hospitals, physician practices, and insurance companies, have adopted value-based care principles to drive improvements in patient care and financial performance. Government initiatives, such as the Medicare Access and CHIP Reauthorization Act (MACRA) in the United States, have supported value-based care and provided incentives for healthcare providers to participate in value-based payment programs.

However, while value-based care has gained traction as a promising approach to improving healthcare delivery, it has also faced criticism from various stakeholders. These critics cite complexity, administrative burdens, inadequate risk, limited cost savings, and unintended consequences such as providers focusing too narrowly on certain quality metrics at the expense of other important aspects of care. Despite these criticisms, many healthcare stakeholders see this as an industry trend and remain committed to advancing value-based care as a means of improving the quality and sustainability of the healthcare system and in positioning the organization for expansion.

POSITION THE ORGANIZATION FOR GROWTH

People thought for centuries that dissecting, reducing, and taking things apart was the best way to learn about them. Scientists examined an entity by analyzing each individual component, further splitting the elements until they could scrutinize the smallest part. This method remained popular until the twentieth century. Then, a new way of understanding began to surface: the systems approach.

In 1952, Ludwig Von Bertelanffy, a theoretical biologist, called this new approach "General Systems Theory." This theory allowed a new way to think about and study the interactive and dynamic alterations of living phenomena. According to Von Bertelanffy, *a system is a structure of an organized set of interrelated and interacting parts that maintain their own balance amid the influences of the environment.*

A system is a collection of parts that interact with each other to function as a whole. If something is made up of several parts that do not interact, and the arrangement of these parts is irrelevant, this is a pile of materials rather than a system. For example, a pile of bricks is a pile of bricks whether we add to it or subtract from it. Cutting it in half gives two piles of bricks and adding to it yields a bigger pile of bricks. Essentially, however, the mound of material remains a mound of material; but cutting a car in half does not produce two smaller cars.

To continue the car analogy, if experts could determine the best parts of each type of automobile, could the world's best car be manufactured by collecting each of these parts and putting them together to make the world's best automobile? Taking the engine from one type of car, a transmission from another model, and a carburetor from yet another would not combine to create a system that worked. The parts would not be compatible and would not operate to make a functioning machine, much less a superlative mode of transportation.

Groups in healthcare are even more complicated; they are *living* systems. Each person can be viewed as a separate segment of the system, but the effect of the interaction among them is more than the sum of the parts. The synergy created by the members and the outputs of the group result in the dynamic relationships of the members who constantly define and redefine themselves, their behavior, and the functions of the group. Combined, the group members, who ideally become a team, can do things that none of them could do separately.

Social scientists, psychologists, and organizational theorists soon began to see systems theory as a way of explaining the complicated dynamics of interpersonal relationships. Peter Senge, author of *The Fifth Discipline,* explained human endeavors as "invisible fabrics of interrelated actions" and observed, "Systems thinking is a conceptual framework, a body of knowledge and tools that has been developed over the past 50 years, to make the full patterns clearer, and to help us see how to change them effectively." Applying this approach to the study of small groups provided an awareness that groups are process-oriented, synergetic, and environmentally dependent.

Viewing any system in terms of its context is the first step to understanding the *synergetic* effect of the system on healthcare organizations. This means that $1 + 1 = 3$, evidencing a system as more than the sum of its parts. Synergy occurs when the group's performance or accomplishments surpass the capabilities of the individual group members. In other words, the team's unique combination of talents, knowledge, and experience is greater than the sum of the individual contributions. The ideas of one member often trigger a response from another person that neither would have thought of independently. The vitality of one individual can spur others on when their energy wanes.

In the mental sense, synergy forms when a type of collective intelligence and shared memory begins to develop as the team matures. Senge described this development as a kind of aligning during which a commonality of direction emerges, and individuals' energies harmonize. He said that a resonance occurs "like the 'coherent' light of a laser rather than the incoherent and shattered light of a light bulb." The team has a commonality of purpose, a shared vision, and understanding of how to complement one another's efforts.

This interconnection of the parts means that all divisions of the structure change when one piece of it changes. When one element alters, all others must adjust to accommodate it if the system is to survive in a healthy state.

This "domino effect" surfaces whenever team members interact because the effects of any action cause consequences to ripple through the system.

To ensure healthcare improvement programs succeed, we encourage our clients to set bolder goals, to equip the best people to do their best work, and to find the money to make it all happen. At the same time, we urge everyone in the organization to develop abundance mindsets and to adopt behaviors that, over time, will reset culture.

Early in our careers, we thought of these as pretty good ideas—and they were. But with time, cracks started appearing in the armor. Instead of focusing attention on the *systems* in which people work, we concentrated on fixing the people. Now we know that the systems need fixing far more than the people do. In general, the healthcare industry owes the changes to frontline clinicians who have shouldered the weight of unoptimized systems to shift the focus to designing systems that facilitate the delivery of the highest-quality care.

Quality and safety, the primary work products of healthcare, have the same job: participating in the effort to *continually improve* the care provided to patients and families. Organizations that have taken this approach consistently weave disparate information and improvement initiatives together into a practical, technology-enabled management system that improves care for patients and reconnects clinicians to their purpose, leading to sustained improvements in many outcomes. Evidence indicates that focusing on the care operating system leads to an improved organizational learning culture and a highly engaged staff that can serve as antidotes to the current crisis of burnout in the health workforce.

Whether executives in a healthcare organization aspire to grow organically or acquisitively, systems matter. If executives don't have the systems to keep their own house in order, why would anyone else want to partner with them?

CONCLUSION

As technology advances, so will concerns about its misuse. Critics have already expressed concerns about altering the human gene pool with unpredictable long-term consequences, such as the creation of "designer babies" that only wealthy individuals and nations will be able to afford, exacerbating existing social inequalities. Many fear the "playing God" element or fundamentally altering nature, thereby causing new health problems or genetic disorders. Of course, we will face supervisory challenges when rapid advancement outpaces regulatory frameworks.

In other words, in the next ten years, we will face the same kinds of challenges and opportunities we've always had. These controversies have led to ongoing debates in scientific, ethical, and policy circles about how to develop and use technology responsibly—and we predict they will continue to do so. Things will be easier, however, if we start anticipating future needs and discern bandwagon trends from healthcare improvements.

Appendix: The Henman–Perkins Healthcare Survey

In our work, we have helped healthcare organizations improve patient care, strategic focus, operational excellence, and staff morale while generating millions of dollars in financial improvements.

To discover how to leverage your strengths and mitigate your weaknesses, score your organization from 1 to 5 for each of the statements below. After completing the survey, simply add your scores to find your total score and the implications for your organization.

1	2	3	4	5
Totally Disagree	Disagree	Not Sure	Agree	Totally Agree

STRATEGY

Mission

1. We know why we exist.
2. We understand the demographics we serve.
3. We know who would miss us most if we went away.
4. Our 3- to 5-year vision is unmistakable.
5. Our strategy changes regularly, but our mission never does.

Vision

6. We have clearly defined one-year goals.
7. Decision-makers agree on priorities.
8. We have established key performance indicators for strategic objectives.
9. We know clearly who our competitors are.
10. We position our services to outrun them.

Culture

11. Ethics guides our behavior.
12. We have created an action-oriented culture that reduces bureaucracy.
13. Clear values govern our behavior.
14. Ignoring these values will get you in trouble, no matter who you are.
15. We agree about the right and wrong ways to do things.

EXECUTION

Technology

16. We have what we need to change and improve.
17. Our approach to telehealth is cutting-edge.
18. We take a fact-based approach to decision-making.
19. Our physicians stay up to date on Electronic Health Record (EHR) systems.
20. We have improved patient care with advanced technology.

Change Management

21. The way we do things is flexible and easy to change.
22. We react well to competitors' changes and other changes in healthcare.
23. We proactively embrace innovation.
24. Different parts of the organization cooperate to create change.
25. We reward innovative thinking.

Patient-Centered Care

26. Patients find it easy to communicate with us.
27. We know what our patients want and need.
28. Patient surveys reflect our commitment to patient-centered healthcare.
29. Patients' comments and recommendations often lead to changes.
30. Our decisions reflect the best interests of the patient.

TALENT

Retention

31. We attract virtuosos who want to work for a thriving organization that has distinguished itself in healthcare.
32. We have the quality of employees to support our strategy.
33. Our performance appraisal system helps us retain the best people.
34. Our compensation/benefits help us attract top talent.
35. We have development/advancement opportunities to attract and retain top talent.

Succession Planning

36. The CEO and other senior leaders support the succession plan.
37. Succession planning is a systematic, transparent process in this organization.
38. When openings occur, whether planned or sudden, we have enough people ready to move up.
39. We have specifically defined success factors for each level from solo contributor to functional leader that are specific to each functional area.
40. We have identified possible successors for each major role.

Team Orientation

41. Candor remains high whether the news is good or bad.
42. Members understand what decisions and tasks others expect them to address.
43. Members address rather than gloss over differences.
44. We have torn down silos.
45. Members share credit and assume merited blame.

FINANCIAL

Leadership

46. We know how to translate our strategy into specific results and activities that deliver the financial outcomes to which we've committed.
47. Leaders model our values.
48. Leaders hold people accountable for driving the strategy.
49. Our leaders' focus is on strategy, and their decisions reflect this focus.
50. We have the leaders we need to drive our strategy.

Reimbursement

51. Our clinical documentation supports our coding/Diagnosis-Related Group (DRG) assignment, as demonstrated by our ongoing audits.
52. Our clean claim rate is consistently at least 90%.
53. We know what our denial rate is, and it does not exceed 8%.
54. Our physician leaders are our partners in strategic planning.
55. Our team does a good job documenting and auditing patient-level data to understand our case mix better.

Growth

56. We know where we make money—and where we don't.
57. We can articulate our competitive advantage/unique contribution.
58. We understand industry trends.
59. Because we tie our mission, vision, values, and strategy together, we execute effectively.
60. Financial rewards are tied to performance that supports the strategy.

SCORING YOUR SURVEY

240–300 Points

Your organization enjoys a superior strategy. You have set a clear direction and have aligned people and processes. You have established a competitive advantage that includes a strong strategy and clear tactics to support it. By responding to patient needs, developing talent, implementing effective operations, and defining sound financial objectives, your organization has acknowledged what it must do to beat the competition and has identified ways to implement this strategy.

The key area of concern for you is to ensure that your strategy remains relevant to the fast-changing healthcare environment. If you start to lose high-potential candidates, however, examine your hiring and management practices.

180–239 Points

Your organization functions at an above-average level. You have a strong grasp of what you should do and have put in place most of the people and processes to make that happen.

Your key area of concern involves maintaining what you have and mitigating your areas of weakness. Spend some time looking at these questions:

- What could our competition do to hurt us?
- What M&A deal would knock us off our feet?
- What do we do to ensure ongoing improvement?
- Do we have people in the pipeline to take the strategy forward?

120–179 Points

Your organization enjoys only a modest understanding of what your strategy should be. Any major change to the healthcare or economic landscape will put you at risk. Similarly, industry changes could knock you off your feet. Examine your decision-makers. Are they strong analytical thinkers? Leaders who can anticipate consequences? People who see the future as open and malleable? If not, scrutinize your bench and see who needs to be replaced.

Organizations like yours often succeed in the short term. Despite current financial success, however, you may lack a strong strategy. You probably engage in effective operations that have accounted for your success in the past, but you've made success somewhat questionable in your future. You may offer good services and be passionate about what you do, but you might lack excellence or profitability.

Members of organizations like yours frequently resist discussions of strategy because what they're doing seems to be working. Perhaps you have a strong commitment to lean processes, Six Sigma, or Total Quality Management, all tactics for driving a strategy. Management makes solving immediate problems their primary focus, and strategy formulation seems like a distraction from that priority. Investing the time in a strategy formulation process will lead you to fewer wasted hours and distracted efforts in the future.

Below 119 Points

You are not making enough healthy decisions, your healthcare organization is in serious trouble, and you don't have too many strengths to leverage. Start by looking at the four major categories: Strategy, Execution, Talent, and Finance to identify which part needs to improve. Chances are it's Talent and Finance. First, you need to examine the decisions and the decision-makers that got you in the position and scrutinize how your finances have suffered as a result. You will probably need to make significant changes to the leadership team and to your reimbursement practices.

Index

Note: *Italic* page numbers refer to figures.

For Product Safety Concerns and Information please contact our EU
representative GPSR@taylorandfrancis.com
Taylor & Francis Verlag GmbH, Kaufingerstraße 24, 80331 München, Germany

www.ingramcontent.com/pod-product-compliance
Lightning Source LLC
Chambersburg PA
CBHW061309220326
41599CB00026B/4796